A Trial of Generals

To my father, who gave me the
strength to question. And to my
mother, who believed.

He that would make his own liberty secure must guard even his enemy from oppression; for if he violates this duty he establishes a precedent that will reach himself.
Thomas Paine

A Trial of Generals

Homma, Yamashita, MacArthur

Lawrence Taylor

Icarus Press
South Bend, Indiana
1981

A TRIAL OF GENERALS
Copyright © 1981 by Lawrence Taylor

The Publisher wishes to thank the Defense Audiovisual Agency (Still Photo Depository) of the U.S. Army, the National Archives, The Library of Congress, U.S. Military Academy at West Point, Wide World Photos, and the United Press International for their assistance in obtaining photographs for A Trial of Generals.

Icarus Press, Inc.
Post Office Box 1225
South Bend, Indiana 46624

Library of Congress Cataloging in Publication Data

Taylor, Lawrence, 1942–
  A trial of generals.

  Bibliography: p.
  Includes index.
  1. War crime trials—Philippine Islands—Manila.
2. Homma, Masaharu, 1887–1946. 3. Yamashita,
Tomoyuki, 1885–1946. 4. MacArthur, Douglas,
1880–1964. I. Title.
JX5441.M3T38   341.6'9'0268   80-27445
ISBN 0-89651-775-6

Contents

Acknowledgments

The following is a true account, taken from official U.S. Army records, trial transcripts, Japanese and American military memoirs, and historical reference works.

While this book has been the result of research based upon many historical sources, the author is particularly grateful to the following individuals for information contained in their respective works: A. Frank Reel, *The Case of General Yamashita*, William Manchester, *American Caesar*, Arthur Swinson, *Four Samurai*, Douglas MacArthur, *Reminiscences*, Frank Toland, *The Rising Sun*, Louis Morton, *The U.S. Army in World War II: The Fall of the Philippines*, And Jonathan Wainwright, *General Wainwright's Story*.

Appreciation is also due to the U.S. Army for providing over seventy-four volumes of trial transcripts, as well as numerous photographs and documents.

Prologue

February 23, 1946

Los Baños is a small town located about thirty-five miles south of Manila. Like so many other small towns in the Philippines, it is little more than a collection of ramshackle huts and weather-worn structures spread haphazardly over a dirty clearing. At its edges, the raging jungle growth fights for control of the town, creeping in from all sides, spreading green tentacles toward the rotting lumber, cracking mortar, and rusting corrugated metal that forms the skeleton of the village. The native Filipinos will soon hack away at the living encroachment with U.S. Army-issue machetes, but the victory will be only temporary; within days, the lush green mass will again be surging into the outskirts of their little town.

At two-thirty in the morning, Los Baños is in a restless sleep, the stupor of the tropical heat and humidity cut by the slight briskness of a breeze that flows down from the cooler mountains nearby. Normally at that dark hour,

1

there would have been a drugged near-silence over the village, a vague murmuring smothered in a blanket of dully droning mosquitoes. Normally, there would have been the occasional faraway cry of a bird from the jungle or the faint rustle of a scrawny, mange-covered dog slowly shuffling down the dirt streets, the distant shriek of a monkey, or a hiss from some unknown thing crawling beneath a house. Normally, this lulling music of the night would be hidden in the blue-black of a starry equatorial sky.

But this is not a normal night. There is a stillness in Los Baños on this night, a strange deadness that has settled over the village. And as if sensing something, the surrounding jungles are hushed, the bird has stilled its song, the monkey does not cry. Above, the stars are veiled in a dull grey haze, and the moon has died hours earlier. This night is black. And silent.

In the town, yellow light flickers from kerosene lamps in many of the dusty houses, shadows playing eerily on the ground. Yet nothing moves. At two-thirty in the morning, lights burn where there were normally none, but there is no sign of life.

On the edge of the village, not far from where the jungle began, a larger, more modern building rises above the surrounding squalor of shacks and deteriorating stores. The building has been freshly covered with a coat of white paint, and the ever-present sprawl of weeds that grew everywhere in the village are nowhere to be seen. A high stucco wall runs from the rear of the building, enclosing what must have been at one time a large courtyard. Strung along the top of the wall are three taut and neatly spaced rows of rusting barbed wire.

The building has only a few windows, all of them unusually small for such a large structure. Each of the windows has thick steel bars forming the black outline of a cross against the light pouring from inside; it is not the softly dancing light of the villagers' lanterns but the steady harsh glare of bare electric bulbs. Occasionally, the light is broken for a second or two by the outline of a man in a uniform, carrying a rifle.

Deep inside of the building, near its center, is a small room with no windows. It too has recently been painted white, and the single light bulb that dangles overhead from the cracked ceiling fills the room with an unrelenting starkness. Only one door leads into the room—steel, with a barred window; though fairly new, the door is already beginning to corrode from the acidic effects of the humidity, and the hinges squeal loudly when the door is opened.

Against one wall is a small steel bed frame covered with a thin mattress that is beginning to show signs of mold; a drab brown U.S. Army blanket is sprung tightly over it, the edges neatly tucked underneath. A small, collapsible field desk is set against the opposite wall, a metal folding chair arranged neatly before it. A white porcelain toilet bowl sits in the corner, cracked and uncovered but cleanly scrubbed.

In the center of the barren room, an older man kneels, his bald head bowed deeply. He is thickly built, broad in the shoulders and chest, with the huge, gristly stomach of the Sumo wrestler. His arms and legs seem to dangle from the short, powerful body as he kneels on the floor. Mounted on the massive shoulders, with almost no neck to be seen, is a cannonball of a head; round, barren of any hair, it seems to jut up from the muscular bulk of his body to a blunt point. The small, flattened nose and thin, slanted oriental eyes give him an efficient, purposeful look. He appears to be about fifty years of age, and he is dressed in a badly rumpled grey suit. The kneeling man could be a gracefully aging Japanese businessman. But he is not.

Another Japanese man, much older and in the robes of

a Buddhist priest, stands before him. He has a shock of white hair about the ears and a long, thin white beard. He is saying something in a quiet, frail voice to the man on his knees. Periodically, the short, stocky man in the grey suit nods slightly.

Suddenly, there is a metallic clanging from the door. The sound of a lock turning, and then the door is swung open, its hinges crying out shrilly. Two soldiers step into the room, wearing the khaki uniform of the United States Army; holsters are strapped to their sides. They part, and another uniformed man steps in, this one an officer. He is young, perhaps twenty-five.

"It's time," the officer says simply.

The kneeling man nods slightly. Slowly, with a surprising grace, he rises to his feet. He smiles to the old priest, then bows deeply. The priest bows in reply, a look of sadness on his face, and then turns and walks out of the room.

The man in the grey suit steps over to the desk. He picks up a single sheet of paper, gazes at it for a moment. His lips are pressed tightly into a thin line, his eyes burning with a deep intensity. He turns toward the officer, hands him the paper.

"Please," he says softly. "Please send my thankful word to Colonel Clarke and Lieutenant Colonel Feldhaus, Lieutenant Colonel Hendrix, Major Guy, Captain Sandberg, Captain Reel at Manila court."

The young officer looks up, nods to the older man. Then he looks at the two soldiers. One of them pulls out a pair of handcuffs, steps behind the man, and carefully locks his wrists together. Almost imperceptibly, the Japanese gentleman draws himself erect, his chin high. He takes a deep breath, then looks at the officer and nods slightly.

The officer steps back as the man marches out of the room, one of the soldiers before him, one following.

When they had left, the officer looks around the room one last time, then steps out into the corridor. Quickly, he walks after the two soldiers and the prisoner.

At the end of the brightly lit corridor, the first soldier turns to the right. The group stops at a large metal door. The officer steps forward, pulls out a ring of keys, and unlocks the door. He opens it and steps out into what appears to be a huge courtyard.

The handcuffed man follows the first soldier out into the inky blackness of the night. He opens his eyes, trying to adjust from the harsh brightness of the building's lights. He stumbles for a moment, then quickly rights himself; again, he throws his shoulders back and walks forward erect and proud.

Very slowly, as he gets further away from the building, he begins to make out shadowy forms. The forms are not distinct yet, not quite recognizable, but he knows well what they are.

"Detail," the officer says in a low voice, "halt!"

The two soldiers and the older man in the grey suit stop. Another uniformed man steps out of the darkness, comes to a position of attention. He returns the younger officer's salute.

The Japanese gentleman looks behind the new officer. There, in the still, humid blackness of the early morning, he can see the outlines of the structure. A high, wooden platform, with a series of steps leading up to it. And at the top, a mounted cross bar with a braided rope dangling down into a noose that hangs in stillness.

"Lieutenant General Tomoyuki Yamashita," the new officer announces, "you have been found guilty of . . ."

The officer drones on, reading the liturgy from memory. But there is no interpreter, and the aging gentleman who stands so erect can understand little of what is being said. It is unimportant. He has made his peace with his god, and he wishes now only to die quickly.

". . . order of General of the Army Douglas MacArthur, Supreme Commander for the Allied Powers." The officer is silent now, staring into the older man's face. He sees no expression there, no fear, no doubt. If there is anything in the stoic face, it is calm, serenity, acceptance.

The officer steps back sharply. "Carry out your orders," he barks.

A soldier steps forward with a black cloth sash and raises it to the handcuffed man's head.

"Please," the Japanese man says. Then he turns to his right, in the direction that he feels Tokyo to be, and bows deeply. He holds the bow for a few seconds, his hands bound behind him. Then, slowly, he straightens and again stands erect, staring straight ahead.

The soldier wraps the cloth around the man's head, covering his eyes, then ties it into a knot. With a soldier at each side, the man walks forward and begins mounting the freshly sawn wooden steps. The new officer climbs behind him.

At the top, the older man takes two steps and then stops. The two soldiers turn him around, then lead him back slightly until he is directly in the center of the trapdoor. They look at the officer, then step back to the edge of the platform.

"Do you . . ." The officer coughs. "Do you have any last words?"

The blindfolded man is silent for a moment. Then quietly, he says, "I will pray for the Emperor's long life and his prosperity forever."

The officer continues staring at him for a moment, then steps back. "The sentence of the court will be carried out."

A tall, thin man who has been standing off to the side now steps forward. He grabs the dangling noose and fits it carefully over the grey-suited man's bare head. Then, quickly, he tightens the rope around the thick, almost nonexistent neck. He maneuvers the knot of the noose to the left side of the man's face. Finished, he steps back.

The aging Japanese man in the wrinkled suit stands alone now in the center of the platform, his back arched, shoulders straight, jaw lifted high.

The courtyard is deathly still, as if time has suddenly stopped in the little country village of Los Baños. The hot, sticky blackness of the night seems a vast emptiness, and the faint outlines of the men on the strange platform an unreal apparition. Nothing moves. Nothing makes a sound.

Suddenly, a shrill squeaking of metal, and a dull explosion of wood against wood. A split second later, a loud thud and a sharp crack. Then, silence again. Silence save for the low, pitiful groaning of rope and timber.

April 3, 1946

It is hot now in Los Baños, a heavy, oppressive heat with no relief from the mountain's cooling wind. Again, the Filipino village lays quietly under the blanket of midnight but this time with a sprinkling of stars overhead. Lights once again flicker from the cracked and peeling windows of the town, and for one more time there is a tense stillness in the air, a strange sense of waiting in the muggy darkness.

Inside the large building, in the same room where the Buddhist priest and the stocky old man had met six weeks earlier, another aging Japanese gentleman now sits at the olive-green field desk. He stares at the cracked texture of the freshly washed white wall, apparently lost in a vast emptiness. Yet his eyes are seeing deep greens and pale blues, vast yellow fields of flowers, and then children, young, laughing children, playing, falling, giggling hysterically. And an old man, stooping in the waving ocean of colors and fresh smells, is picking up one of the children, up high onto his chest, holding her close, laughing with her, smelling the sweet, clean hair. And under a gnarled black tree near them, a slim, delicate woman, with years in her eyes but an infinite grace in her movements, kneels on a spread blanket. Almost shyly, she smiles and looks down, her soft, aging beauty stabbing into the old man's chest as she gently tucks the edges of the silk kimono around her legs.

There is a very slight smile on the man's face as he looks down from the wall and resumes writing on the sheet of paper spread out before him on the desk. His deep black eyes, more occidental in shape than Japanese, are glistening from the faint veil of wetness; they are soft eyes, gentle, concerned eyes that reflect a deep sadness within. Thin, sensitive lips move slightly, as if he were talking with someone as he wrote.

Like the tenant of the starkly barren room before him, he is a big man, broad at the shoulders and powerfully built. But this man is tall, much taller than his countryman, rising to over six feet. And he carries this towering height almost regally, with grace and yet with a kind of humility. Like the tenant before him, he wears a rumpled grey suit, which seems ludicrously small on his tall frame, the sleeves pulling up above his wrists. And yet he rises above the meanness of the clothing, his handsome features and almost aristocratic bearing overpowering the grey rags.

This aging Japanese gentleman seems a study in contradictions. Tall, proud, powerful, clearly a man of command—yet filled with gentleness, sensitivity, and a deeply agonizing doubt. Oriental, yet occidental. A soldier, yet a poet. An artist in the body of a blacksmith. But it is in his eyes that the conflict is most reflected: gentle, questioning eyes, the hurt eyes of an infinitely wise child trying to understand.

He puts his pen again to the paper, and the ornate script slowly forms.

> Don't lose courage, children! Don't give in to temptation. Walk straight on the road of justice. The spirit of your father will long watch over you. Your father will be pleased if you will make your way in the right direction rather than bring flowers to his grave. Don't miss the right course. This is my very last letter.

The man looks up again at the cracked wall in front of him, again sees the softly porcelain face of the older woman. His slender lips again move slightly. Then, slowly, he turns the sheet of paper over and resumes writing.

> My Dear Fujiko:
> Twenty years feel short but they are long. I am content that we have lived a happy life together. If there is what is called the other world, we'll be married again. I'll go first and wait for you there but you mustn't hurry. Live as long as you can for the children and do those things for me I haven't been able to do. You will see our grandchildren and even great-grand-children and tell me all about them when we meet again in the other world.
> Thank you very much for everything.
> Masaharu.

As he finishes the letter, the clanging and the rusty squeaking of metal signal what he knows to be the end. He looks up to see the two American soldiers and the young officer standing awkwardly near him, waiting. Behind them, an older officer in uniform stands quietly; a Bible is in his hands and the chaplain's insignia on his collar.

Slowly, the Japanese gentleman folds the paper and hands it to the officer. The officer nods, not looking at him. He places the folded letter in his pocket.

The old man rises from the chair, then turns and smiles at the three Americans. He waves to a tray on the bed containing sandwiches and bottles of beer. "Please, gentleman," he says cheerfully, "join me. This is a good time."

He hands a beer to one of the soldiers, another to the young officer. Awkwardly, they accept. The two soldiers look at each other, then down at the floor in silence. The old man grabs another bottle and raises it in toast. "Here's to all of you," he says, his eyes dancing, almost joyful. "Please congratulate me on the start of a new life."

He drinks deeply from the beer, then puts the bottle back on the tray. The soldier and the officer sip from the bottles, unsure of themselves. Somehow, they had reluctantly come to respect and even like this tall, gentle man, this enigma from another world. Could he really have done all the things they said he had done?

The man places his large hand on the young officer's arm. "I am ready," he says.

One of the soldiers pulls out a pair of chrome handcuffs, coughs self-consciously. Then he links the Japanese gentleman's wrists behind his back.

Once again, the slow parade of prisoner and soldiers leaves the cell and proceeds down the harshly lit corridor, their heavy steps echoing in the empty hollowness. The chaplain walks beside the tall erect man, saying nothing.

Again, the officer unlocks the big metal door, and the small group marches out into the wet, warm darkness of the night. The handcuffed man looks up at the blue-black sky, smiles slightly as he sees the ocean of phosphorescence spread across the heavens.

They march across the courtyard to the far wall. There a single wooden pole stands in loneliness. At the pole, the men stop. One of the soldiers unlocks the handcuffs, then coughs again nervously. Nodding in understanding, the tall man in the ill-fitting grey suit backs up against the pole, places his arms behind it. The soldier again handcuffs him, binding him to the thick wooden stake.

The young officer looks at the old man, suddenly embarrassed. "Are there any last words, sir?"

The old man smiles, shakes his head.

Slowly, the officer pulls out a strip of black cloth and raises it toward the man's face. He would never forget the look in the old gentleman's eyes just before the blindfold was in place: an acceptance, a sad calm, yet with a touch of disappointment, of confusion, of hurt.

The two soldiers and the officer quickly march across the courtyard. The chaplain says a few hushed words at the tall gentleman's side, then also withdraws.

Standing thirty feet in front of the man bound to the pole is a neat row of American soldiers, rifles held rigidly to their sides. They are evenly spaced, rod-straight in a row, facing the blindfolded man. There are eight of them, all young; one of them, a baby-faced private who is blinking rapidly now, could be no more than seventeen.

Another young officer stands to their side. His voice suddenly breaks the humid stillness. "Detail, atten-shun!"

The eight soldiers snap to brittle attention.

"Ready!"

Eight rifles leap from the ground into the air.

"Aim!"

A clatter of steel and wood and a slightly uneven row of barrels level themselves at the tall, proudly erect man.

"Fire!"

The brilliant flash of oranges and yellows, the deafening concussion of the explosions, and, quickly, the smell of gunpowder as grey smoke slowly rises above the young men.

The tall gentleman is bent forward now, sagging to the side as the handcuffs bite into the dead flesh. He is swaying gently as the heavy silence of the night again settles over the village.

Book One:
Bataan

1
War Plan Orange

THE CHOICE WAS CLEAR.

By the middle of 1941, Japan had been cut off from all raw industrial materials by the economic sanctions imposed by the governments of the United States, Great Britain, and the Netherlands. The embargo would clearly cripple the Japanese economy and eventually leave Japan defenseless against the attacks of a major power, such as Russia. Tokyo had to make a critical decision, a decision with far-reaching implications—surrender plans of expansion into Southeast Asia and China and thereby placate the Allied Powers, or invade British and Dutch possessions and take the needed strategic materials by force. This second course meant war with Great Britain and the Netherlands. More importantly, it would probably mean war with the United States—even if American territory were not attacked.

The British Empire was dying and that of the Netherlands almost dead. But the United States remained a young, vibrant, powerful force in the Far East. It was the United States, then, that Tokyo knew must be reckoned with. It was the United States that stood between Japan as a small, overcrowded island and Japan as the Asiatic power she felt destined to become. And it was in the Philippines where the United States held its strategic foothold, blocking Japanese expansion.

The Philippine nation is an archipelago of approximately 7,000 islands extending over a distance of a thousand miles, from just south of Taiwan (then called Formosa) to the north of Borneo. Strategically, the island group was centered directly in the heart of the Far East and lay directly across any path leading from Japan to the rich supplies of oil and raw materials in Southeast Asia and the East Indies. Although 5,000 miles from Hawaii, Manila lay only 700 miles from Hong Kong, 1,500 miles from Singapore; Tokyo itself could be easily reached by a bomber squadron from the Philippines. Clearly, no nation could hope to control Asia without first controlling, or at least neutralizing, the Philippines.

The Philippine archipelago, then, was the key to Japan's ambitions. Yet it lay in the hands of an American government determined to oppose Japanese expansion that would threaten the holdings of the Allies in the Far East. Seized from Spain during the Spanish-American War, the islands had immediately injected the United States into Asia as an imperialist power. The Filipinos had eventually been granted a measure of autonomy, and in 1934 the Tydings-McDuffie Act was passed in Washington, providing for Philippine independence in 1944. But the act specifically stated that during this ten-year transitional period the United States would be permitted to "maintain military and other reservations and armed forces" in the islands and would have the power "to call into the service of such armed forces all military forces organized by the Philippine Government." In 1941, then, the Philippines was still an American stronghold.

The American-controlled Philippines lay directly in the path of Japan's imperialistic plans. Tokyo must decide to either attack the Philippines or abandon Japan's glorious destiny.

The key to the defense of the Philippines lay in the abilities of one man: General Douglas A. MacArthur. A brilliant tactician, politically adept, and a leader of proven courage, MacArthur had been recalled to active duty in July of 1941 to serve as the commander of the U.S. Army Forces in the Far East. With his headquarters in Manila, General MacArthur was instructed by Chief of Staff General George Marshall to reinforce the Philippines' defense "in view of the possibility of an attack."

The selection of MacArthur for the job had been a wise one. No one knew more than he about the Philippines, and no one was more convinced that the islands could be successfully defended against the Japanese. He had written in the *Christian Science Monitor* in 1938 that the central island of Luzon (containing Manila) had "only two coastal regions in which a hostile army of any size could land. Each of these is broken by strong defensive positions which, if properly manned and prepared, would present to any attacking force a practically impossible problem of penetration." He went on to write that "it would be a matter of serious doubt whether an enemy could concentrate superior forces at any vital Philippine area," and that any Japanese blockade would be impractical without the unlikely agreement of the other nations present in the Far East. And to a news correspondent, MacArthur had confidently predicted that if Japan entered the European war, the Allies could defeat her with half of the military forces then present in the Pacific: "The Japanese navy would be either destroyed or bottled up tight."

MacArthur had more than a nodding acquaintance with the people and the land of the Philippines. In fact, he was considered by some in Washington to be an imperious, self-proclaimed savior of the Philippine nation, a messiah convinced that he was destined to lead the Filipinos into the twentieth century. More than one military leader or politician felt that his loyalties were stronger to Manila than they were to the United States.

MacArthur's deep involvement with the Philippines went back many years. His father, the famous Major General Arthur MacArthur, Jr., had fought the guerrilla "Nacionalistas" in 1899. Like his son, General Arthur MacArthur had a reputation for tactical brilliance and bravery under fire. And like his son, his personal mannerisms were often objectionable. His own aide, Colonel Enoch H. Crowder, later said, "Arthur MacArthur was the most flamboyantly egotistical man I had ever seen, until I met his son." But Douglas MacArthur's father was effective. In one bloody campaign after another, he had slowly swept the guerrillas from central Luzon, finally defeating them on a peninsula on Manila Bay called Bataan. The location of the elder MacArthur's victory was to supply some irony in his son's battles many years later.

One of the rebels who had surrendered to MacArthur's father on Bataan was a young mestizo, Major Manuel L. Quezon. And it was Quezon who, thirty-four years later, traveled to Washington to discuss the formation of the new Philippine Commonwealth under the Tydings-McDuffie Act. Although elections had not yet been held, Quezon was the overwhelming favorite for the presidency.

Quezon soon ran into the son of the American general to whom he had surrendered on Bataan. Douglas MacArthur was at that time the chief of staff of the Army and was about to retire from his military career to pursue the study of law; he was noted for his political acumen, and a law degree would prove helpful for any future aspirations.

Quezon learned of MacArthur's plans to retire and asked him if the Philippines could defend itself once it received independence. "I don't *think* the Philippines can defend themselves," MacArthur replied. "I *know* they can."

Even more impressed now with the confident chief of staff, Quezon asked President Roosevelt to consider assigning MacArthur to the Philippines as a military advisor. Roosevelt agreed, and in July of 1935 MacArthur arrived in Manila with the new title of "military advisor to the commonwealth government." He was instructed to aid in the "establishment and development of a system of National Defense" and was given unusually broad powers. He was authorized to deal directly with the secretary of war and the new chief of staff and "in all cases not specifically covered" to act on his own best judgment. He was instructed that "your mission must be accomplished [but the] way and means are largely left to you."

MacArthur was now acting in an independent capacity as Quezon's advisor. Although he took with him a staff of American officers that included a Major Dwight D. Eisenhower, he was essentially a civilian. The U.S. Army command in the islands was called the "Philippine Department" and was totally separate from the Philippine government's army. Yet the commander of the Philippine Department, Major General Lucius R. Holbrook, was instructed that assisting MacArthur was "the most important peacetime mission of your command."

MacArthur had, of course, realized the potential value of his position. He would soon become invaluable to Quezon and to the Philippine people. And he had important connections in Washington. His objective was to be appointed governor-general of the Philippines, the highest-ranking American position in the islands. Robert Taft had once held the office, and it was presently occupied by Frank Murphy. When the new constitution was adopted by the Philippine people, the position would be called "high commissioner." MacArthur lost no time lobbying extensively for the position, spreading disparaging facts about Murphy, while lining up his own influential contacts. Finally, at a dinner with Roosevelt, MacArthur was promised the position.

MacArthur's plans were temporarily thwarted, however, since the law would not permit the appointment of a man on active duty with the army. Nevertheless, MacArthur convinced Roosevelt to enact special legislation overcoming the technical obstacle. It was about this time, however, that Murphy heard of MacArthur's campaign and began loudly protesting. At last, Roosevelt decided to preserve the status quo, leaving Murphy as high commissioner and MacArthur as military advisor.

This was to be only a temporary setback in MacArthur's plans. In the following years, he was to apply his theatrical genius to winning for himself a place of prominence in the islands that he was slowly coming to adopt as his home.

MacArthur had immediately established a headquarters in Manila. While his military entourage took over much of the red-roofed Manila Hotel on Dewey Street, MacArthur had taken for himself the six-room, air-conditioned pent-house atop the hotel. From one balcony, the entire city of Manila could be seen spread out below; from the other, opening dramatically off of the formal dining room, was a breathtaking view of Bataan and Corregidor across the bay. The penthouse was lushly furnished in polished mahogany, maroon leather, and deep red velvet; Chippendale, Chinese, and French provincial mixed freely. Signed photographs of important political and military figures adorned the walls, and valuable books, art objects, and souvenirs collected by Mac-

Arthur and his father were displayed everywhere. Mac-Arthur's office-home was half museum, half palace.

In the closets, MacArthur kept a huge supply of clothing—over two dozen uniforms and suits alone. Most of the suits were grey-checked or white tropical, usually accompanied by a silk shirt, bow tie, and tan-and-white shoes. But it was the uniforms that MacArthur was known for. As his air corps chief, Major General Lewis H. Brereton, later noted, "He is one of the best-dressed soldiers in the world. Even in the hot topical climate of Manila, where we wore cotton shirts and trousers which for most people became wet and wilted in an hour, I have never seen him looking otherwise than if he had just put on a fresh uniform."

Nor was MacArthur's uniform to be limited to the khaki of the U.S. Army. On August 24, 1936, President Quezon's wife presented him with a gold baton, officially bestowing upon him the title of "field marshal." Accordingly, MacArthur designed a special uniform for himself consisting of black trousers and a white coat garnished with layers of medals, gold cord, and a cap braided heavily with gold, which was to become as familiar to the world as his later corn-cob pipe and dark glasses.

Eisenhower said that he had tried to "persuade MacArthur to refuse the title since it was pompous and rather ridiculous to be the Field Marshal of a virtually non-existing army." He was later to learn that the idea had not come from Quezon but had actually originated with Mac-Arthur himself. It was from this moment that relations between MacArthur and his assistant, now a lieutenant colonel, soon became strained.

MacArthur was now the highest-paid professional soldier in the world. He was still on the U.S. Army active list, receiving a salary as a major general. In addition, he was being paid $33,000 a year from the Philippine gov-

ernment for his services as military advisor and "field
marshal." Many Americans were revolted by the swag-
gering histrionics, calling MacArthur "the Napoleon of
Luzon"; some even saw sinister dictatorial designs in his
conduct. But to the Filipinos, Douglas MacArthur was a
hero and an inspired leader who commanded respect and
even awe. His dramatic flair captivated their imagination,
and his colorful swagger appealed to their more primitive
nature. Unpopular with the American community in Manila though he may have been, the Filipinos nevertheless
loved him; his distant aloofness inspired the child-like
confidence of a father figure.

Whatever MacArthur's personal faults or egotistical
ambitions, he was the man for the job. His demonstrated
brilliance in strategic planning qualified him to establish
the defenses for the islands, and his ability to lead men
and command the respect and faith of the Filipino population were critical to the success of those plans. Washington would back his decisions and provide sufficient
funding and supplies. Could his influential contacts out-
weigh the growing number of his enemies? Men like
Marshall, once under MacArthur's command and ban-
ished by him to the Illinois National Guard, recognized
his abilities but suspected his motives.

When MacArthur took over as military advisor in Manila, he was confronted with the seemingly insurmountable problem of defending a coastline longer than that of
the United States. Yet, as always, he expressed confidence. In a speech in 1936, he said he planned to create a
defensive force of such strength as to make an invasion
so costly in lives and money that "no Chancellory in the
world, if it accepts the opinions of the military and naval
staffs, will ever willingly make an attempt to willfully
attack the Philippines." The islands had "enormous defensive advantages," MacArthur said: their geographic

isolation, their mountainous character, their heavy forests and jungles, their narrow beaches. When he was finished developing the Philippine Army and the coastal defenses, MacArthur said, the islands would be strong enough to oppose successfully "any conceivable expeditionary force."

The raw materials for MacArthur's plans were supplied by a combination of American funds and equipment, advisors and units from the U.S. Army's Philippine Department, and the National Defense Act of December 21, 1935. This National Defense Act was the first legislative measure passed by the newly formed Philippine National Assembly, and embodied a plan specially created by MacArthur. It provided for a regular army of 10,000 men, backed by a reserve force which was expected to reach 400,000 within ten years—i.e., by 1946. Conscription was begun, a military academy established, and the island divided into ten military districts.

MacArthur's plans, reflected in the act, provided for no navy but rather for an "Off Shore Patrol." Perhaps indicative of MacArthur's disdain for the relative importance of a navy, the plan envisioned a small fleet of fifty or so PT boats. "A relatively small fleet of such vessels," MacArthur reasoned, "manned by crews thoroughly familiar with every foot of the coastline and surrounding waters, and carrying, in the torpedo, a definite threat against large ships, will have a distinct effect in compelling any hostile force to approach cautiously and by small detachments."

Military leaders in Washington considered this laughable; the Japanese had more destroyers than MacArthur would have PT boats, or "Q-boats" as he called them, and in any event such a small number of little boats could not begin to cover the thousands of miles of coastline. MacArthur replied that the absence of a traditional naval force was because of the defensive nature of the objective. The purpose of a large navy, he said, was to protect overseas possessions, and since the Philippines had no colonies, the only naval job was inshore defense. Inshore defense, he continued, could be provided by "flotillas of fast torpedo boats, supported by an air force," which would prevent an enemy force from getting close enough to Philippine beaches to land troops and supplies.

Despite objections in Washington, MacArthur remained adamant, and the boats were ordered from a British firm. Unfortunately, MacArthur's theory was never to be tested: only three boats had been delivered by December 7, 1941, joined by six existing PT boats from the U.S. Navy.

In addition to a huge reserve army and a mini-fleet, the National Defense Act provided for the development of a Philippine Army Air Corps. Air bases were to be built, pilots trained, and fighter and light bombers purchased.

MacArthur was slow in beginning implementation of the plan. The initial draftees, numbering around twenty thousand, did not reach the training camps until 1937. It then developed that these recruits spoke eight different languages and eighty-seven dialects. The enlisted men of one unit might speak a Bicolanian dialect, while its officers spoke Tagalog; the American army instructors could speak neither, nor could their recruits understand English. On top of this, a significant percentage of the draftees were illiterate; many of these were to become clerks or quartermasters.

Discipline immediately became a problem in the new Philippine Army and remained one until the outbreak of war resulted in the adoption of courts-martial. As the military academy would take four years to produce its first class, there was a critical shortage of officers. Training facilities and equipment were almost unheard of, and when the Japanese invaded in 1941 many Philippine Army units went into battle without ever having fired a shot in practice.

Supplies too were scarce. Most of the "soldiers" wore tennis shoes, an ill-fitting blue fatigue suit, and a pith hat. Helmets were unavailable, and the men were armed with World War I-vintage British Enfield and American Springfield '03 rifles. Usually, the wooden stock on the rifles was too long for the small Filipinos, and the weak metal extractors were easily broken and not replaceable.

The mainstay of MacArthur's new Philippine Army, then, was poorly equipped, poorly organized, poorly trained and poorly led. As one American advisor noted at the time, the Philippine soldier seemed to be proficient in only two things: "one, when an officer appeared, to yell attention in a loud voice, jump up and salute; the other, to demand three meals per day."

Despite the slow progress in developing the Philippines' forces, MacArthur remained adamant in his confidence that the islands could be successfully defended against a Japanese attack. It would take the Japanese a half-million men, three years, and $5 billion to take the Philippines, he said, and they wouldn't be willing to pay that price. Furthermore, he argued, England's disastrous Gallipoli campaign of World War I proved conclusively that amphibious exercises were too dangerous to risk. Many critics pointed out that Luzon alone had over 250 miles of possible landing beaches, but MacArthur was convinced that any landing attempted by the Japanese would be foolhardy and easily repelled.

Corregidor alone, MacArthur emphasized, was "the strongest fortified point in the world" and was, for all practical purposes, impregnable from attack. And Manila could not be held without taking Corregidor. With his 1946-projected army of 400,000 Filipinos, his hard-hitting armada of PT boats, and a small air force of fighters and bombers, MacArthur was convinced he could beat off any Japanese attack. Nor was he forgetting that the United States would not stand idly by: The Philippine Division of the U.S. Army would prove helpful, and the

Pacific fleet—together with the British and Dutch naval forces—would quickly decimate the Japanese Navy.

Never, as the thirties came to a close, did MacArthur express any doubts as to the outcome of a Japanese invasion of the islands. Such an invasion would, simply, prove an expensive disaster to Japan. Many historical analysts have suggested that MacArthur's bravado, so hollow in perspective, was consciously created to bluff Japan into holding off an attack. Yet MacArthur seemed convinced by his own rhetoric; his private conversations, his personal attitudes, reflect that he was absolutely sure a Japanese attack would be successfully repelled. Even his racial chauvinism toward the Japanese misled him: When MacArthur observed how skillfully the Japanese combat planes were flown in the opening days of the war, he assumed that the pilots were Caucasian. He seemed to share in the image of the Japanese prevalent in prewar America and the Philippines: They were little, yellow-skinned people with poor teeth and bad eyes—a comic race that could never stand up to red-blooded American or Filipino soldiers.

Yet despite MacArthur's continued confidence, President Quezon was growing worried. And as he grew worried, he grew more distant from his beloved "field marshal." The two men had become very close after MacArthur had arrived in Manila. In 1937, MacArthur had married Jean Faircloth; a son was born to them in 1938, Arthur MacArthur, IV, and Mr. and Mrs. Quezon were made his godparents. The president considered the general his *compadre*, almost a brother. None of this, of course, hurt MacArthur's future personal plans. But now China was being overrun by the Japanese, yet Quezon had been told by MacArthur that Chiang Kai-shek's forces were too strong to defeat. Would the Philippines be next? Was MacArthur wrong about the islands' defense also?

In July of 1938, Quezon went to Tokyo without his American military advisor. There he discussed the Japanese intentions and the plans of the Filipino people with Japan's diplomats. When he returned, he began demanding that the United States escalate the plans for Philippine independence; the country should be autonomous by 1940, he said, not 1944. When Washington refused, Quezon cut the defense budgets, saying that building up the Philippine Army would only serve to antagonize Japan.

MacArthur's army began to shrink, and morale declined even further among the troops. The two men rarely talked with each other anymore, and Quezon even spoke to the newest high commissioner of dismissing MacArthur as military advisor. Perhaps the low point in the relationship came when Quezon told a huge audience in Manila that "it's good to hear men say that the Philippines can repel an invasion, but it's not true and the people should know it isn't." The islands, Quezon told the crowd, "could not be defended even if every last Filipino were armed with modern weapons." Shocked when he heard of this, MacArthur went to Quezon's secretary and asked for an appointment; he was curtly told that Quezon was too busy to see him.

It was about this time that Eisenhower asked to be transferred out of MacArthur's command. His request was granted. Eisenhower's replacement, Colonel Richard K. Sutherland, proved a totally different kind of man. Like MacArthur, he was ambitious and soon ingratiated himself as MacArthur's closest advisor. One newspaper correspondent characterized him as "brusque, short-tempered, autocratic and of a generally antagonizing nature." He was known for his oft-repeated view that, in wartime, democracy should be abolished and a dictatorship proclaimed in the United States. This was the man who was to become MacArthur's chief of staff and closest advisor.

It was 1940, and MacArthur's position was not envi-
able. On the one hand, his direct boss, the president of
the Philippines, had become alienated and continued to
speak in defeatist terms. On the other, his enemies in
Washington seemed successful in having blocked exten-
sive funding or major shipments of supplies. The Philippine Army was growing large but was pitifully trained
and supplied, even more poorly led and disciplined. His
navy and air corps were still largely on the drawing
boards, and the only effective fighting force in the islands, the U.S. Army's small Philippine Department with
its crack native but American-led Philippine Scouts, was
under the command of another general. And Japan was
clearly on the move, with MacArthur's Philippine Islands
squarely in her way.

In the spring of 1940, the situation began to change
rapidly for MacArthur. To begin with, an old friend, Major General George Grunert, had just been appointed to
the command of the Philippine Department. Together, he
and MacArthur begged Marshall to supply more American troops and supplies and urged the taking of a hard-
line stance against Japanese demands. Grunert agreed
with MacArthur that the Philippines could be defended.
Washington began to listen to him; they assumed that it
would be he who would lead American forces should
hostilities break out. MacArthur, of course, had no intention of giving up that role to Grunert.

MacArthur particularly objected to the official plan of
defense for the Philippine Islands. Known as *War Plan
Orange*, it had been drafted by the joint army-navy
leaders in 1938 as one of many defense plans coded by
color; the Orange plan was to be used in the event of an
emergency in which only Japan and the United States
were involved.

War Plan Orange assumed that a Japanese attack would come without declaration of war and with less than forty-eight hours warning. Reinforcements, therefore, would not be possible for a considerable period of time—the defense would have to be conducted by the Philippine Army and any U.S. forces present. An updated analysis of the plan in July of 1940 resulted in an estimate that the Japanese would send about 100,000 men to capture Manila and its harbor defenses, supported by heavy air and naval fire. They would probably land on numerous beaches at the same time, thus spreading out the defending forces. The attack, according to War Plan Orange, should be expected to come during the dry season, shortly after the rice crop was harvested—in December or January.

The mission of American and Philippine forces under the plan was to hold the entrance to Manila Bay—the best and most strategic harbor in the Pacific—and deny its use to the Japanese Navy. Only central Luzon, therefore, was to be defended; the rest of the archipelago was to be forfeited. Enemy landings should be initially contested and, failing in that, enemy forces that did land were to be eliminated. If the enemy gained a successful foothold, the plan went on, U.S. forces should fight a delaying action. All this was, however, subordinate to the primary mission, the defense of Manila Bay. Bataan was considered necessary to control of the bay, and an orderly withdrawal to the Bataan peninsula, together with fortifications on Corregidor Island, would prevent Japanese use of the harbor. Bataan was the key. It was to be defended to the "last extremity."

The supply plan of War Plan Orange was a complicated one. Provision had to be made for withdrawing supplies into Bataan sufficient to last 31,000 men for 180 days. Corregidor was similarly to be supplied with enough rations, materials, and ammunition for 7,000 men to last six months. By then, it was felt, the American navy would have fought its way across the Pacific and resupplied and reinforced the defending forces. Thus strengthened, the Philippine units could counterattack and drive the Japanese into the sea.

So War Plan Orange stated. But in 1940 few military leaders in Washington believed this would happen. Naval officers theorized that it would take at least two years for the Pacific fleet to fight its way to the Philippines. Nor was there a plan existent for a concentration of men and supplies on the American West Coast for shipment to the islands. In simple truth, army planners felt that when supplies were exhausted on Bataan and Corregidor after six months, the garrisons would go down in defeat. Yet nothing was said of this; everyone hoped that if and when such an attack came, some plan could be improvised to rescue the men stranded 7,000 miles across the Pacific.

It was against this plan that MacArthur now railed. War Plan Orange was defeatist in concept, he complained. What was needed was an aggressive plan aimed simply at one thing—destruction of any enemy that dared invade the Philippines. Not merely Manila should be defended but the entire archipelago.

MacArthur's optimism, backed now by General Grunert, proved contagious. Perhaps because Washington simply wanted to believe, perhaps because MacArthur's facts and figures began to make sense, high officials in the War Department began to feel that just maybe the Philippines *could* be defended. Or, what was even better, maybe a buildup in strength in the Philippines would scare the Japanese off. There were many flag officers who believed that shipments of the new B-17 bombers, proving so effective by the British against the Germans, would now change the picture; the Japanese, it was felt, would hesitate before attacking the Philippines when they realized the B-17s could blast the ships out of the water, then bomb Japan herself. The performance of the bombers seemed to justify the hope that the South China Sea could be successfully blockaded by air and that the Philippine Islands could be made into a "self-sustaining fortress."

For whatever reason, MacArthur's long-espoused views of defending the entire Philippines became increasingly accepted in high circles. On February 1, 1941, MacArthur wrote directly to his old enemy, Chief of Staff Marshall. War Plan Orange was pointless, he wrote; the Philippines must be defended as a "homogeneous unit." He informed Marshall that he would very soon have 125,000 troops ready to take the field, with supporting warplanes and a naval force "whose primary striking element will consist of from thirty to fifty high-speed motor torpedo boats." He wrote that he could "provide an adequate defense at the beach against a landing operation of 100,000, which is estimated to be the maximum initial effort of the most powerful potential enemy."

Soon after this, MacArthur sent a note to an old friend, Steve Early, Roosevelt's press secretary. In it, he suggested that Early discuss with Roosevelt the possibility of MacArthur's appointment as commander of all forces in the Philippines, American and Filipino.

Still, nothing happened. Finally, on May 29, 1941, MacArthur wrote a letter to Marshall stating that he was going to shut down his office of military advisor and return to San Antonio; MacArthur forwarded a copy of the letter to Early.

This time MacArthur got action. The War Department had wanted Grunert named as Supreme Commander, but Roosevelt decided on MacArthur. On June 20, Marshall advised MacArthur that he and Secretary of War Stimson had "decided that your outstanding qualifications and vast experience in the Philippines make you the logical selection for the Army in the Far East should the situation approach a crisis."

The "crisis" took place one month later. On July 22, 1941, Japan occupied southern Indochina. The Philippine Islands were now almost completely surrounded by Japanese forces. MacArthur was recalled to active duty on July 26 with the rank of major general, his permanent rank before retirement at the end of 1937; two days later he was promoted to lieutenant general.

MacArthur was now confronted with a number of tasks. He had to reorganize his command, merging the Philippine Army and the U.S. Army's Philippine Department into one structure—the United States Armed Forces of the Far East. Then he had to accelerate the drafting of men into the Philippine Army, as well as their training. Finally, he had to obtain needed supplies and reinforcements from Washington.

The first job was quickly accomplished, with Colonel Sutherland being appointed as MacArthur's chief of staff. The U.S. Army forces in the Philippine Department consisted of 22,532 men, 11,972 of which were Filipinos—American-trained members of the elite Philippine Scouts. The largest single army unit was the Philippine Division, commanded by Major General Jonathan M. Wainwright; most of the men in the unit were Scouts. The second largest unit was harbor defense under Major General George Moore, headquartered at Fort Mills on Corregidor; most of these were artillery men.

These U.S. Army units were merged with the existing units of the Philippine Army. At the time of MacArthur's takeover, the Philippine Army numbered approximately 80,000; by December, it would number over 120,000.

Meanwhile, unknown to MacArthur, strategic war plans were being drafted during secret talks between American and British officers. The result was the U.S.–

British Commonwealth Joint Basic War Plan, later referred to simply as *Rainbow 5*. The basic premise of the Rainbow plan was that American strategy in the Pacific would be strictly defensive; Germany and Italy would be the initial primary objectives.

Quite simply, Rainbow 5 meant the forfeiture of the Philippines, as well as Guam and Wake Island, to the Japanese. While not as severe as earlier plans promulgated by the U.S. War Department's War Plans Division—withdrawal of all U.S. forces in the Pacific to a line extending from Alaska through Hawaii to Panama—the Rainbow strategy was unacceptable to MacArthur. There was no intention to evacuate the Philippines, but neither were there to be any plans to reinforce them. MacArthur's confidence that the defense of the islands was both plausible and necessary was, apparently, not shared by Rainbow's drafters.

Upon hearing of Rainbow, MacArthur immediately contacted Marshall and objected to the plans for the Philippines. The "citadel" concept of defending only Manila, and only with existing forces, was too "negativistic." MacArthur claimed he could keep the Japanese out of the islands altogether and thereafter launch counterattacks against Japanese shipping and even against Japan herself. He was convinced, MacArthur said, that the Japanese attack would not come until April of 1942—the old War Plan Orange prediction of a December invasion was unrealistic—and that by then he could block any amphibious assault anywhere in the islands. He would, he continued, soon have a force of approximately 200,000 men organized into eleven divisions, as well as a strengthened air force. With this force, any Japanese attack could be repelled, no matter where in the islands it came. "The strength and composition of the defense forces projected here," MacArthur claimed, "are believed to be sufficient to accomplish such a mission."

Surprisingly, Marshall accepted MacArthur's views. He informed MacArthur that a revision of Rainbow as it related to the Philippines was being drafted, and joint board approval was expected. Marshall then advised his own staff that it was now the War Department's policy to defend the Philippines: Rainbow 5 would be accordingly amended. He wrote MacArthur that increased reinforcements and massive supplies would be quickly forthcoming. Most importantly, shipments of B-17s were considered critical to the defense of the islands. The sudden "realization" that the Philippines could be effectively defended had the effect, Secretary Stimson later noted, "of making the War Department a strong proponent of maximum delay in bringing the Japanese crisis to a climax. . . . In their eyes, the Philippines suddenly acquired a wholly new importance and were given the highest priority on all kinds of military equipment."

MacArthur quickly advised his staff of the new defense tactic—the beaches "must be held at all costs," he said. Despite his earlier assertion that Luzon's beaches yielded but two possible landing spots, now, he said, no matter where in the unending miles of coastline the invasions came, the American and Filipino forces were "to prevent a landing." In the event any Japanese forces reached the shore, they were "to attack and destroy the landing force."

Singlehandedly, then, General MacArthur had altered the Allied strategy of defense in the Philippines. Critical supplies and manpower would be forwarded to the islands, and the entire archipelago was to be defended. But this was taking a terrific risk, a risk that was to prove fatal. MacArthur would gamble, first, that he could meet the invasions no matter where they occurred along the thousands of miles of beaches. And he would gamble, second, that he would defeat them on the beaches. And it was a gamble. If MacArthur failed to beat the Japanese at the waterline, then he would have to retreat back to Manila, back onto Bataan peninsula. In essence, he would have to revert to the old War Plan Orange.

But in such a retreat, there was one very serious drawback: Unlike War Plan Orange, there would be no supplies for six months on Corregidor or Bataan awaiting the men. The supplies would be spread throughout the islands, ready for use in meeting the enemy's landings. What supplies would be available for transfer to Bataan and Corregidor after a retreat would be an unknown quantity, dependent more on luck than anything.

The die was cast. The fate of the American and Filipino soldiers was now sealed.

With the news that his defense plans would be approved, MacArthur immediately began reorganizing his forces to carry out the more difficult mission. He broke his army into four units: the North Luzon Force, under General Wainwright; the South Luzon Force, under Brigadier General George M. Parker, Jr.; the Visayan–Mindanao Force, under Brigadier General William Sharp; and the Reserve Force, in Manila, directly under his own command. Each of the commanders was instructed that, in contrast to War Plan Orange, there was to be "no withdrawal from beach positions"; the beaches were to "be held at all costs."

Washington wasted no time in sending supplies and reinforcements. In fact, MacArthur even turned down a National Guard division, saying he already had one U.S. Army division and ten Philippine divisions. "Equipment and supply of existing forces are the prime essential," he told Washington. "I am confident if these steps are taken with sufficient speed that no further major reinforcement will be necessary for accomplishment of defense mission." The reinforcement of the islands was now accorded the War Department's highest priority. As a result, requests from MacArthur for supplies during the following months received instant approval. "I wish to express my personal appreciation for the splendid support that you and the entire War Department have given me along every line since the formation of this command," he wrote Marshall. "With such backing the development of a completely adequate defense force will be rapid."

Manila soon began to fill up with antiaircraft guns, tanks, heavy artillery, ammunition, howitzers, machine guns and supplies of every description. In West Coast ports and Honolulu, shipping schedules were set up that recognized the priority of the Philippines over Hawaiian defenses.

Most importantly, the warplanes came. Eighty-one modern P-40 fighters arrived by ship. And in September, nine Flying Fortresses completed a historic 10,000 mile flight from San Francisco to Clark Field in the Philippines via Midway, Wake, Port Moresby, and Darwin. Soon after, twenty-six B-17s flew from Hawaii to Clark Field.

By the end of November, MacArthur could count 35 B-17s in the islands and 107 P-40s. This represented more than half of all heavy bombers in the U.S. armed forces and one-fifth of all the fighters. MacArthur now had a total of over 250 warplanes of all types—considerably more than were based in Hawaii—and more were on the way.

Nichols Field, just outside Manila, was soon filled with fighters and dive-bombers. Clark Field, sixty-five miles to the north, was quickly modified to accommodate the new superbombers, as was Del Monte Field 500 miles to the south on Mindanao.

The naval forces of the U.S. Asiatic Fleet under Admiral Thomas C. Hart were now headquartered in Manila. The fleet consisted only of a heavy cruiser, a light cruiser, thirteen World War I–vintage four-stack destroyers, and seventeen submarines. In addition, Admiral Hart had twenty-four PB4 patrol aircraft and miscellaneous gunboats, minesweepers, and tankers. Attached to Hart's command was the U.S. Marine Corp's 4th Regiment, currently based in Shanghai; by December, most of the marines had successfully been transferred by gunboats to the Philippines.

By the end of December, after the attack on Pearl Harbor, MacArthur's force was reaching impressive proportions and growing larger every day. He could boast an army of over 130,000 men and the largest complement of modern combat aircraft on any military base in the world. The islands were bristling now with cannon, tanks, and antiaircraft guns. Corregidor commanded Manila Bay, virtually impregnable to attack, and the islands were laced with an intricate network of defenses.

Yet behind the apparent readiness were two major weaknesses. First, the vast majority of the army consisted of Filipinos who were poorly trained, undisciplined, and badly led. Second, MacArthur's plan attempted the impossible: the defense of a coastline longer than that of the United States with little or no provision for strategic withdrawal.

Nevertheless, MacArthur expressed unguarded confidence to Washington. Marshall had reflected MacArthur's optimism during a secret press conference in Washington on November 15. He had then informed the reporters that war was imminent but that the situation in the Philippines was excellent. General Douglas MacArthur had been given "the greatest concentration of heavy bomber strength anywhere in the world," he told them. After had had succeeded in defending the islands, MacArthur would conduct bombing raids on Japan and obliterate her "paper cities."

The stage was set. MacArthur was convinced that the attack would not come until the following April, and privately he was gearing the training, dispersion, and supply of his forces on that belief.

On November 24, 1941, Admiral Hart was told by Washington that an agreement with Japan was unlikely and that recent Japanese troop movements indicated that "a surprise aggressive movement in any direction, including attack on Philippines or Guam was a possibility." Three days after this, the War Department sent a stronger message to MacArthur and the Army commander in Hawaii: "Negotiations with Japan appear to be terminated. . . . Japanese future action unpredictable but hostile action possible at any moment . . ."

At the same time, the Navy sent an even stronger wire to Admiral Hart, which Hart relayed to MacArthur: "This dispatch is to be considered a war warning . . . . An aggressive move by Japan is expected within the next few days." The Philippines, Thailand, and Malaya were named as the most probable places for attack.

MacArthur cabled back that "everything is in readiness for the conduct of a successful defense."

The first days of December 1941 were tense ones for the Philippines. MacArthur's planes noticed heavy Japanese ship movements toward Malaya; unidentified aircraft were detected over Luzon. And MacArthur was beginning to think that possibly he had been wrong about the timing of the attack. As late as November 27, he had assured Hart that the existing alignment and movements of Japanese troops had convinced him that the invasion would not come before the spring. But Hart continued to feel otherwise.

Then, on December 6, MacArthur suddenly ordered the North Luzon Force to be ready to move quickly to its assigned positions on the beach. He informed his air commander that a full air alert was in effect and that all aircraft should be dispersed and placed under guard. Corregidor was put on full alert.

On Sunday, December 7 (it was December 6 on Hawaii's side of the date line), the atmosphere relaxed somewhat. That evening, a party was thrown by the 27th Bombardment Group for General Brereton, complete with "the best entertainment this side of Minsky's." At the party, Rear Admiral William Purcell, Hart's chief of staff, commented to Colonel Sutherland that "it was only a question of days or perhaps hours until the shooting started." Sutherland agreed. Later that evening, Brereton instructed his staff to place all air units on combat alert as of the next morning, December 8.

As the men danced and drank into the night, a relatively small force of 43,000 Japanese soldiers sat quietly in the darkness of eighty-five troop transports steaming south from Formosa. This was the 14th Army, commanded by Lieutenant General Masaharu Homma. With this force, Homma had been ordered to defeat MacArthur's 130,000-man army and conquer the entire Philippines. And this was to be accomplished within fifty days.

2
The Poet General

MASAHARU HOMMA WAS FIFTY-FOUR YEARS OLD WHEN HE embarked on the invasion of the Philippines, a tall, handsome man with dark, clear-cut features. He was a quiet individual, almost withdrawn, and appeared distant and aloof even by the standards for a general of the Imperial Army. Yet, oddly, his temperament was that of the artist—emotional, sensitive, easily hurt, and with a deep need to be loved. In fact, many of his fellow officers felt there was something vaguely feminine about Homma. They recognized his genius as a strategist and admired his proven courage and natural ability to lead men. But they could not understand this man who composed verses in the middle of battle, who labored long hours in writing dramatic plays, who spoke of painters and sculptors and collected fine period furniture. And they remembered the tragic series of reckless love affairs in the years before he married Fujiko, the almost comical romances that were the joke of the military world in Tokyo. Yes, Masaharu Homma was something of an odd fish, one Japanese general observed—brilliant, yet slightly unstable; aristocratic, yet unpredictable; calm and cool, yet deeply passionate.

Homma was born on November 27, 1887, on Sado Island off the northwest coast of Japan, to a wealthy landowner. While he was still a boy, his father died, leaving him to be raised by his elegant, socially prominent mother. Mrs. Homma took her husband's death very hard and never fully recovered. Increasingly, as Homma grew older, she dwelt on the memory of her dead husband, neglecting her only child. Relatives and social acquaintances noted that she spoke more of her long-dead husband than she did of her son. And it was in this environment of cultured wealth and deep loneliness that Masaharu Homma gradually matured into manhood.

When he reached fifteen years of age, Homma had to decide what career to choose. His mother was still wealthy and well connected in political circles, yet he decided to reject the path of aristocracy and chose instead the spartan life of the soldier. The one thing his mother and dead father could not give him to help him in his career choice was a *samurai* tradition, and perhaps for this reason Homma took the entrance examinations for the military academy.

Homma scored high on the tests and was quickly accepted. At the academy, his academic brilliance and leadership abilities began to show themselves. By the end of his training, he was recognized as a genius, a man to watch. At the critical final examinations, his fellow students watched in nervous awe as Homma finished the tests and walked out of the room long before anyone else. Soon after, the tall, quiet young man graduated from the academy at the head of his class.

Homma was assigned to duty with an infantry regiment as a second lieutenant. After distinguishing himself there, he received the honor appointment as attaché to Prince Chichibu, the youngest brother of the emperor.

During his tour as military attaché, Homma met and quickly fell in love with a beautiful girl named Toshiko Tamura. Her father was an army general, but her mother had been a *geisha* in Akasaka. He wanted desperately to marry the girl, but he knew that his aristocratic mother would never agree to a marriage with the daughter of a geisha. His closest friend from the military academy, Hitoshi Imamura, advised him to exercise caution. Army officers had to be very careful whom they chose for a wife, as any kind of scandal could destroy even the most promising career. Nevertheless, Homma insisted that he must marry her. He could not help himself, he told his friend; he loved her too much to let her go.

Homma approached an old family friend, General Sohruku Suzuki, and asked him to serve as the matchmaker. The idea of romantic love was quite foreign to Japanese life, and General Suzuki was opposed to the marriage. But he had been like a father many times to Homma, and reluctantly he agreed. In keeping with the rigid Japanese customs, he decided the amount of money to be given by the groom to the bride for buying her trousseau and new furniture, and he arranged the wedding with the members of Toshiko's family. Finally, despite the pleas of his mother and friends, Homma married the woman he loved. Soon, the couple was blessed with two children.

Then in 1914, Homma was sent to the staff college, an honor reserved for those thought to have the potential to eventually become generals. Again, Homma excelled in all phases of the training, particularly in the theoretical battle problems called TEWT (Tactical Exercises Without Troops), then in great favor with the British Army. He was noted for his tremendous concentration on the tactical problems, often staying up all night with maps and charts before coming up with solutions that were drafted in clear, powerful, and elegant language. So impressed were the instructors at the college that many of his reports were forwarded to Imperial Army Headquarters for review, and one of his defense studies eventually became a standard for use throughout the army.

When Homma graduated with honors from the staff college, he was assigned to a British Army unit at Oxford, England. It was 1918, and World War I was still raging in Europe. Homma served as an observer with the British Expeditionary Force, accompanying them through the battles of France and finally into Germany.

It was about this time that Homma received a tragic letter from his mother. She wrote that she had received a telegram from his wife, Toshiko. In the letter, Toshiko told her that their two children would be arriving at Sado Island on a boat and asked her to please care for them for a while. The elder Mrs. Homma had met the children at the dock, finding them to be very upset and crying, and had taken them to her home. Then she had received a second letter: Toshiko wrote that it was impossible to raise children in Tokyo on the money an army captain was paid and that Mrs. Homma would have to raise them. Homma's mother had then investigated and discovered that money was not the real problem: Toshiko had become a prostitute. "I hate to give you this bad news, but cannot make it a secret anymore," she concluded the letter. "Please write to your matchmaker and ask him to advise and supervise your wife."

Homma went into a deep depression. He rented a small hotel room in the Mayfair section of London and commenced drinking heavily. Normally a nondrinker, it was not long before he was sprawled unconscious on the floor.

While in a stupor, Homma sent a telegram to Imamura, who had been assigned to embassy duty in London. His friend hurried over to the hotel room; when he arrived, he found Homma crying bitterly. Suddenly, Homma screamed out, "I don't want to live," and lunged across the room at the open third-floor window. Imamura quickly grabbed his legs, but the much larger Homma was too heavy to pull back in. Slowly, Homma began slipping out of his grasp. At the last minute, the owner of a restaurant, hearing the screaming, rushed up to the room and helped pull the sobbing Japanese officer back in.

For the next few hours the two old friends talked. Finally, Imamura advised Homma to follow his mother's suggestion: call General Suzuki and arrange for a divorce.

The next day, Homma did the opposite. He wrote a long, tearful letter to the general, once again declaring his deep and passionate love for Toshiko. He begged him to persuade her to give up her new life, to return to him and the children.

General Suzuki wrote back to Homma in blunt language: "What a weak character you are! Are you really a Japanese officer? Take your wife back now and everyone will laugh at you." Homma quickly replied, "I don't mind being laughed at. I just want her back."

But the situation was beyond any hope, and Homma finally had to accept the fact that Toshiko was gone. Reluctantly, he agreed to divorce proceedings. Then, to the anger and humiliation of his friends and relatives, he quietly bowed to the unreasonable demands of Toshiko's lawyers, giving her almost all of the wealth he possessed. When Imamura asked him why he had done such a stupid thing, he replied, "I have paid for the funeral of my love."

Soon after this incident, Homma was assigned to duty with the 1st battalion of the British Army's East Lancashire Regiment. From there, he was next assigned to the general staff of the British East Indian Army in India. Finally, in

December of 1925, he returned to Japan as a major, assigned to the staff of Imperial Army Headquarters.

During this period of time, Homma's stock as a military officer rose steadily. His genius was widely recognized, and his future appeared to be bright. He was spoken of in high circles as a young man who would soon be a general, a man who would perhaps some day rise to political leaderhsip. His aristocratic heritage and his brilliance as a military leader marked him as a man of destiny.

But marring this sterling career was Homma's unending series of romantic affairs. To the continuing despair of his family and friends, Homma had gone from one tragic love to another. Soon, his poorly hidden romances became the subject of common gossip throughout the entire officer corps of the Japanese Army. To these officers, satisfied with a dull but respectable marriage and content to seek compensation in sake and the periodic services of a prostitute, Homma's endless search for a deep, passionate love seemed ridiculous, laughable.

It was at the end of an affair with a nineteen-year-old geisha girl that Homma finally met the woman he had been searching for. Another old friend of his from the academy, Shozo Kawabe, introduced him to a young woman named Fujiko Takata. At twenty-one, Fujiko was fifteen years younger than Homma. She had already been married—to a college professor—and divorced, and she came from a respected family. She had traveled widely, having spent long periods of time in the United States. Like Homma, she was a gentle, cultured person and had adopted many Europeans ideas.

Homma quickly fell in love with the gentle, quietly dignified Fujiko. She knew nothing of the army and found the women of the *samurai* families as strange as they found her. Homma's friends and relatives advised against further involvement, saying she was simply not a proper wife for an army officer. But Homma was deeply, happily in love, and soon the two were married. His military associates shook their heads, counting the marriage as just another in the eccentric officer's long line of personal disasters.

But the marriage was a happy one from the beginning. The two unlikely partners had found in each other what they had been looking for. The deeply sensitive artist, cast in the unlikely role of a military leader, had finally found the lasting love he had so earnestly desired.

After his marriage to Fujiko, Homma was a changed man. From the security he found in her understanding, he was now able to channel his energies toward his military career. Gone were the impetuous searching, the frantic affairs, the drunken sobbing. Now Homma felt a whole man, with a purpose in life. He still enjoyed writing poetry and plays, but these he would now share quietly with Fujiko.

And Homma's career began to realize the bright promise that had seemed threatened by disappointment. Once again he was sent to London, this time as a full colonel. He attended the disarmament conference at the League of Nations. Then, in 1933, he was assigned the command of the 1st Infantry Regiment in Tokyo. This was considered the best assignment in the Imperial Army, certain recognition that an officer was destined for promotion to general rank; Tojo himself had commanded the regiment just four years earlier.

In 1935, Homma was promoted to the rank of major general. In view of his recognized literary talents, he was assigned to Imperial Army Headquarters to take over the Army Propaganda Department. The Sino-Japanese conflict had erupted, and the army wanted their view given to the world.

For Homma, it was a rare chance to vent his literary abilities, and he threw himself into the job. He personally wrote articles and even songs glorifying the expansion into China. Nor was it a distasteful job to him: Like most others in Japan, Homma believed in the destiny of his nation as an Asiatic power. But he was strongly pro-British and pro-American, and he now saw the war with China as an opportunity to direct the necessary expansion against China and Russia, rather than against the colonies and protectorates of the United States and the European powers.

It was, in fact, this attitude that eventually led Homma to grief. For Homma, a general now with a glowing reputation in Imperial Army Headquarters, was widely recognized as a moderate. More importantly, he was considered the leader of the minority pro-Western faction, a small group of army officers that opposed the idea of conflict with Great Britain or the United States. Yet the Imperial Army was increasingly coming under the control of radical officers anxious to throw the foreign powers out of Asia. And in the intricate political maneuverings for power that continually went on in the army, Homma's firm stand against war with the West was to make many important enemies—among them, General Hideki Tojo.

To understand the events that were soon to take place in Asia, it is necessary to review briefly the political structure of Japan's army.

The Imperial Japanese Army grew in the twentieth century to play a central and directing role in the life of Japan; this was a natural result of Japan's *samurai* history. By 1930, the army had three groups vying for control: the *Sakura-kai*, or Cherry Society, which planned to grab more power for the army at the expense of the political parties and industrialists; the *Kodo-ha*, or Imperial Way, whose purpose it was to establish military rule under the emperor's control; and the *Tosei-ha*, or Control Faction, whose leaders wanted control of the nation and war with China.

The decade of the thirties in Japan was a long history of conspiracies, assassinations, and coup attempts by the three groups, each maneuvering to gain control of the army. And superimposed on this battleground, the struggle between the army and other elements continued for control of Japan herself. Eventually, the Control Faction was to gain hegemony, with Tojo as its leader.

Early in his career, every Japanese military officer had to decide whether he would involve himself in political intrigue or not. If he did not, he might be passed over in promotions; if he did, he might rise quickly—or be ruined just as quickly. The destinies of all officers were to be determined by the political machinations at Imperial Army Headquarters.

Homma had many friends in important governmental positions, and he moved easily in the high society of Japan. Yet, unlike so many of his brother officers, he steered clear of political intrigue. Nevertheless, because of his already elevated status in the army, his views quickly thrust him into a position as leader of the pro-Anglo faction. As such, he was never reluctant to let his views be known, regardless of whom he antagonized, but he shunned any of the political maneuverings that were rampant in the officers' ranks. In fact, his only recorded political activity appears to have been his violent opposition to the appointment of Tojo as vice-minister of war. He was convinced that Tojo's appointment would lead to war with America, and when he heard of it he rushed to the palace and tried vainly to convince his influential friends to oppose the move. But it was too late. Everything was too late. The Control Faction had gained power, and Tojo was now directing the destiny of the Imperial Army—and thereby Japan—on a collision course with the Western nations.

Homma found himself quickly transferred out of head-quarters and into the war in China. But as the commander of the 27th Division, he was soon able to solidify his reputation as a brilliant tactician and a courageous leader of men. Still, he was in disfavor with the new leaders of the army, and when his mission was accomplished, he was kept in China as commander of the Tientsin Defense Army, charged with putting down domestic riots and insurrections. The British still had interests in China, and relations with the Imperial Army had been strained. Fortunately for Homma, however, an old friend of his from London days, Major Francis Piggott, was in command of British troops, and the strain was eased considerably through their mutual trust and understanding.

In December of 1940, Homma was again transferred, this time to take command of the army in Formosa. Soon, however, some of his subordinates began sending secret communiques back to Homma's enemies in Tokyo: Homma was cold, withdrawn, uncommunicative, overly intellectual. He spent all of his time alone in his office, they reported, studying intelligence reports and piles of papers. Rarely did he come out except to attend conferences. He did not travel around the island, reviewing his troops, but kept to himself. He was losing contact with the officers and men in his own command, they said; he was a "paper genius," with no grasp on the realities around him.

While such reports were obviously slanted to diminish Homma's stature back in Tokyo, there was much truth in them. Homma did continue to isolate himself from his subordinates, shutting himself off in his own world of abstract problems and tactical theorizing. More and more, he grew to rely upon his subordinate officers, becoming oblivious to the reality of what was happening in his own command. It was a serious flaw in his abilities as a military leader. It was to prove a tragic flaw on Bataan.

Meanwhile, Tojo's faction had taken complete control of the army and had finally succeeded in exercising the dominant influence over Japan's leaders. Now, as minister of war, Tojo directed that plans for war with the United States, Great Britain, and the Netherlands be drafted. In May of 1941, the overall strategy began to take shape. By November, the plan had been completed and preparations made to launch simultaneous attacks against the Allied-controlled territories.

The immediate objective was to capture the rich Southeast Asian possessions held by the British and Dutch, thus gaining the oil and raw materials needed to continue the war. To take these areas, the threat of the United States in the Pacific had to be eradicated. This meant neutralization of the U.S. Pacific Fleet at Pearl Harbor, breaking the transoceanic line of communications by seizing Wake and Guam and, most importantly, the conquest of the Philippines. The Philippine Islands were not only central to the entire Southeast Asia and East Indies area; they constituted a dagger aimed directly at Japan's heart.

Having neutralized the American presence in the Pacific and seized critical points in Southeast Asia and the Dutch Indies, the Japanese forces would then take the strategic islands of the Pacific, thus forming a perimeter defense across the Pacific. At the same time, the army would spread through the remainder of Southeast Asia, China, Manchuria, Korea, and the East Indies. The result would be a vast triangle, stretching from the Kuril Islands near Russia down to the Solomons and New Guinea off Australia, across to Burma, through China, and up to Manchuria and Korea.

This was to be a war of limited, clearly defined objectives. Imperial Headquarters realized that they could not defeat the United States, and no plan was ever drawn up for that purpose. The initial objectives—Pearl Harbor, Wake, Guam, the Philippines, Malaya, Thailand, and

Hong Kong— were to be accomplished by simultaneous attacks on X day.

The forces required to execute this ambitious plan were carefully calculated. As of December 1941, the Imperial Japanese Army consisted of fifty-one divisions, organized into area commands spread throughout the Far East. Most of these were needed as garrison units in the recently occupied lands of Manchuria, Korea, Formosa, Indochina, and the home islands. Therefore, only a small fraction of the army's total strength would be available for the attacks.

The Southern Army was organized on November 6, 1941, under the command of General Count Hisaichi Terauchi. Terauchi had been war minister in 1936 and was a close ally of Tojo's in the Control Faction. His assignment was to seize the Philippines, Malaya, and the Dutch Indies. He was given command of the 14th, 15th, 16th, and 25th Armies, consisting of ten divisions and three brigades. The 16th Army was to capture the East Indies; the 15th would take Thailand; the 25th would attack Malaya and Singapore; and the 14th was assigned to conquer the Philippines.

Critical to the entire plan, of course, was the seizure of the Philippines. Failing in this, the United States would have a central stronghold from which to strike at Japan's far-flung and thinly held possessions—not to mention the ability to strike at the homeland itself.

The general plan for the Philippine campaign called for air attacks against American planes and fields followed quickly by the amphibious landing of advance army units at Aparri, Vigan, and Legaspi on Luzon and at Davao on Mindanao. These units would seize the airfields, enabling the Japanese airplanes to land and continue operations. When most of the American planes had been destroyed, the main force of the 14th Army would land on two different beaches—at Lamon Bay, southeast of Manila, and along Lingayen Gulf, north of Manila. The major battle was expected to be fought around Manila; once the capital was captured, Corregidor was to be assaulted and taken.

The plan called for the conquest of the Philippines in fifty days. After this period, half of the 14th Army, as well as the air units, would be withdrawn where they were expected to be badly needed elsewhere; the remainder of the 14th Army would be used to occupy the Philippines. It was essential to the success of the plan, therefore, that a complete victory in the islands be achieved by the end of January 1942.

This plan was based on a detailed knowledge of the Philippine Islands, including a fairly accurate analysis of the military forces and fortifications there. The Philippine Army was estimated at about 110,000 men, a figure Imperial Headquarters calculated accurately would be increased to 125,000 by X day. But the Japanese held the Filipino soldier in low regard: he had little endurance or sense of responsibility, it was felt, and was decidedly inferior to the American as a soldier. They were more concerned with the U.S. Army garrison, thought to number about 22,000 including the Philippine Scouts. The Americans were good soldiers, the Japanese believed, but they were inclined to deteriorate physically and mentally in a tropical climate.

Imperial Headquarters felt that the 14th Army, consisting of 43,000 proven and well-led troops, would be sufficient to defeat a combined American-Philippine force three times larger.

The Japanese planners also had amazingly accurate estimates of MacArthur's naval and air forces. The bombers were identified at Clark Field, and the pursuit fighters at Nichols Field; the naval forces were correctly considered to be relatively negligible.

The accuracy of the Japanese information was not an

accident. For months, even years, before the plan was drafted, Japanese spies had been keeping careful notes, mapping coastlines, and taking photographs of installations. As of 1940, in fact, over 30,000 Japanese citizens were residing in the Philippines; many of them were working under a subterfuge, assigned by Imperial Headquarters to gather data. Yet they appeared to be harmless businessmen, servants, and tourists. "Only later," one Filipino officer later reflected, "did I discover that my gardener was a Japanese major and my masseur a Japanese colonel."

There was, however, one flaw in Japanese intelligence. Imperial Headquarters believed that the American–Filipino forces would make their last stand trying to defend Manila and when defeated would scatter and be easily mopped up. Thus, no plans were drawn up for a possible withdrawal of the enemy to the Bataan peninsula. And Bataan was considered a simple, outlying position of no special significance.

On November 2, 1941, Homma, Tomoyuki Yamashita, and Homma's old friend Hitoshi Imamura were ushered into the office of the chief of staff of the Imperial Japanese Army, General Sugiyama. Each of the three men was a senior lieutenant general, and each was considered to be among the most outstanding military leaders in the army.

Calmly, Sugiyama informed them that in a few weeks Japan would be at war with the United States and Great Britain. He eyed Homma casually, observing the tall officer's reactions; there was none. Sugiyama and Homma had clashed before. As an outspoken member of Tojo's Control Faction in earlier years, Sugiyama had more than once exchanged heated words in front of fellow officers over Homma's pro-Anglo leanings. In fact, there had been opposition to awarding Homma such a critical assignment as Sugiyama was about to give him, but it was

indisputable that Homma was perhaps the most brilliant
strategist in the Imperial Army. Still, Sugiyama did not
trust Homma.

Each of the three generals, Sugiyama continued, would
receive key commands in the coming confrontation.
Imamura would be given the 16th Army, charged with
taking the Dutch East Indies. Yamashita, the 25th—Malaya and Singapore. And Homma would be assigned the
critical task of directing the 14th Army against MacArthur
in the Philippines. Briefly he outlined the strategies for
each of the three campaigns, the forces available, and the
expected enemy strengths.

Sugiyama expected Homma to react as the others had,
speaking in formal terms and expressing humble gratitude at being selected for such an important mission. But
when Homma spoke, it was not in the voice of humility
and gracious deference.

"This figure of fifty days," he said thoughtfully, "how
has it been arrived at?"

Taken aback for a moment, Sugiyama replied, "By the
General Staff."

"But on what information?" Homma pressed on. "Has
there been a complete intelligence study of enemy forces,
dispositions, and equipment? Have you taken into account American troop movements in progress now?
Also, I would like to ask, why is the 14th Army being
allotted only two divisions? Who exactly decided that
such a force would be sufficient?"

Still surprised, Sugiyama began to reply in vague
terms. "The General Staff, after a detailed review of the
situation. . . ."

"The fact is," Homma interrupted, "we don't really
know the probable strength of the enemy. So isn't it quite
unreasonable to ask me to take Manila with two divisions
in fifty days? In my view, the target date should be de-

cided after the intelligence survey has been completed, and the general situation studied in light of it."

Imamura sat in his chair, stunned. His old friend was talking back to the chief of the staff, one of the most powerful men in Japan. Surely, Homma's comments would be relayed back to the Ministry of War. And Tojo was known to be looking for an excuse to remove the brilliant but erratic general; Homma had made no secret of his opposition to the impending war, nor of his opposition to Tojo personally.

"Whatever your opinions may be," Sugiyama replied slowly, growing angry now, "the fifty-day period is an integral part of the strategic pattern for the entire Pacific campaign. The figure is firm, and you will have to accept it."

But Homma continued pressing his superior. "Without accurate intelligence as to the enemy forces, how can I undertake to capture Manila in fifty days?"

"You're not the only one facing difficulties," Sugiyama replied, his face growing red. "Everyone is in the same position."

"Can I have some more troops to create a reserve?"

"No. We have none available." He studied the tall figure for a brief moment. "Is the command unacceptable to you?"

"Certainly not. But I cannot undertake to capture Manila within a certain period."

At this point Imamura stood up and tried to ease the situation. To his friend, he explained that he was not being asked to give guarantees. He had only been given a target date, and as a soldier he should simply do his best to meet it; no one could do more.

Yamashita joined with Imamura, assuring Homma that no one expected him to do more than was possible.

Slowly, Homma and Sugiyama settled down, and the

meeting proceeded to other matters. But when it was over, Imamura and Yamashita confided to Homma that they understood why he had stood up to Sugiyama's unrealistic expectations. They were considering doing so themselves, they told him.

In his office, Sugiyama was still fuming over the confrontation. "A Japanese officer should be filled with pride and joy to be offered such a command," he growled to a member of his staff. "What a man to ask questions like that!"

As events were soon to show, Sugiyama was not about to forget Homma.

Meanwhile, Homma's anger over the unrealistic demands was not finished. Back at his headquarters in Formosa, he went over the battle plans with his personal staff. And again the numbers rose up at him: 125,000 Filipinos, 22,000 U.S. Army, heavy bomber and fighter concentrations, mountainous terrain, Corregidor fortress . . . to be taken in fifty days! With only two divisions—43,000 men! Was it possible the General Staff really believed MacArthur's superior force would be so ineffectual? Again, the rage surged up in him as he pointed out the points of landing on the map to his staff.

General Masami Maeda looked up at Homma. Would not the American strategy be to hold out as long as possible, he asked, while the fleet and armies at home could be reorganized? If this were true, would not MacArthur withdraw to the Bataan peninsula rather than try to defend Manila? Bataan was composed of mountainous terrain and jungle surrounded on three sides by water. The Americans would have only one front to defend, with no coastal roads to supply the attacking Japanese forces.

Homma listened to Maeda in silence. He realized there was much to what his general said. Theoretically, at least, such a huge American–Filipino force could hold out indefinitely on the Bataan peninsula, assuming the earlier stockpiling of sufficient supplies. But he also realized that he was expected to follow the plan of attack laid out by Sugiyama.

That evening, Homma dispatched a coded cable to General Sugiyama:

1. What is the true objective in attacking the Philippines? To occupy Manila or destroy the enemy forces in the field?
2. If it is to destroy the enemy forces in the field, it must be realized that this may not be possible in Northern Luzon. The main battle may take place in the Bataan peninsula.
3. If the main battle develops on the Bataan peninsula, the forces of the 14th Army will be insufficient to bring it to a successful conclusion. Forces similar to those allocated for Malaya or the East Indies will be necessary.

On the following day, Homma received a curt reply from Sugiyama: "The main purpose of the attack on the Philippines is the occupation of Manila which is not only the political capital but a place of military importance. The troops opposed to you are third class and unworthy to face us in battle. If therefore they retreat to Bataan, there is no reason why you should not blockade them there."

3
The Battling
Bastards

THE PHILIPPINES WERE LOST IN THE OPENING HOURS OF the war.

At 3:30 on the morning of December 8 (Philippine time), Manila's radio programming was suddenly interrupted with the message that Pearl Harbor was under attack by the Japanese. Colonel Sutherland heard the announcement and immediately called MacArthur in his penthouse. Ten minutes later, MacArthur received a second call—this time from Washington, confirming that the Japanese planes had attacked Hawaii.

MacArthur assumed at the time that the Japanese near Hawaii would be quickly crushed, but he also believed that the main attack would come on the Philippines. But he was ready. Quietly, he awaited reports of the first attempted landings.

At nine-thirty in the morning, American reconnaissance planes observed a group of Japanese bombers heading toward Manila. General Brereton quickly ordered fighters into the sky, but the Japanese bombers changed course and avoided contact.

At ten o'clock, MacArthur learned the stunning news: the Japanese had achieved an overwhelming victory at Pearl Harbor, seriously crippling the U.S. Pacific Fleet. MacArthur could not believe it; everyone had been on battle alert, everyone knew a strike was coming somewhere. How could it have happened?

At a quarter to eleven that morning, reports came into headquarters of a huge formation of Japanese planes approaching Clark Field, where most of the critically important B-17s were based. Once again, as he had done twice already that morning, General Brereton, MacArthur's air corps commander, asked MacArthur for permission to put the entire fleet of B-17s into the air, sending them to Formosa to bomb the Japanese air fleet there. He realized, as did the Japanese General Staff, that the B-17 wing represented MacArthur's ace-in-the-hole. With it, he could sink Homma's convoys before they could reach the Philippines and then launch devastating counterattacks. But again MacArthur remained silent.

At 10:15 in the morning, an armada of almost two hundred Japanese bombers and Zeros took off from Formosa. By noon, they were over Clark and Iba fields, strafing and bombing the B-17s and P-40s sitting helplessly on the landing strips. Within minutes, the attack was over. MacArthur had lost over half of all his air power in the islands. The largest single concentration of American air power in the world had been decimated. And the Japanese had lost only seven fighter planes in the process.

Without the bombers and fighters, the Philippines was now a sitting duck. A critical, almost incomprehensible, mistake had been made, and the islands were now defenseless from the air. If Brereton had been permitted to attack Formosa, it would have been the Japanese airplanes that would have been destroyed on the ground; most importantly, the American bombers would have been saved. Later, after the events had passed, MacArthur denied knowing anything about General Brereton's repeated requests; they had been directed to Colonel Sutherland, he claimed, and he had never received them. Yet he failed to ever explain why he had not taken steps on his own to protect the invaluable bombers.

MacArthur had now made two serious mistakes in his defense of the Philippines. First, he had canceled War Plan Orange, gambling everything on defeating the enemy on the beaches; he was convinced he could achieve the impossible task of defending over two thousand miles of coastline. Second, he failed for reasons still not known to protect his desperately needed air corps from a known attack. In addition, MacArthur had overestimated the abilities of his untested and poorly trained Philippine Army, while seriously underestimating the quality of the veteran Japanese soldier. The combined effects of these errors would normally have been crippling; against General Homma, they were about to prove fatal.

On board one of the transport ships a few days later, Homma sat on the rolling deck writing a poem. A small, slightly built man studied him from a distance. Hidemi Kon, a novelist drafted as a war correspondent, wrote down his thoughts as he watched the general compose verse under the early morning skies. He was well above normal height, Kon wrote, with sloping shoulders, large, distinctive eyes and long eyebrows. He seemed to be a man "made for command." He joked easily with his men, yet Kon sensed that he was under some great personal strain. Then Kon saw it: This was a man of wit and culture, he later reflected, a deeply sensitive man imprisoned by the iron straitjacket of army discipline. An artist, an individualist, a nonconformist—and yet forced to accept the rigid structures of the *samurai* code.

Kon watched as a group of soldiers cautiously approached their general. Bowing obediently, one of them asked Homma if he would please write a song for them to sing in the coming battle. Homma smiled, obviously pleased at the request. Within minutes, he had written a verse:

> *Great birds over the sea*
> *Great eagles over the land*
> *Ranging their silver wings*
> *Fly toward the southern sky.*
> *Swiftly they capture Nielson Field;*
> *Clark Field they destroy at a single blow.*
> *Where is the Sky Fortress?*
> *Where is the shadow of the P-40?*
> *What a splendid action in the enemy sky!*

The soldier bowed again, thanked the general for the song. Then the small group drifted away, leaving the tall, silent man alone on the deck, staring at the shadowy outline of the Philippine Islands just now taking form on the blue-black horizon. He looked back at the long line of transport ships, then at the sleek destroyers on their flanks. Again his eyes strained for the shadowy coastline.

The convoy had earlier been bombed by the few remaining American B-17s, but there were not enough of them to do any serious damage. And with most of the P-40s destroyed, the bombers had been open to attack from the Japanese Zeros.

Meanwhile, the invasion was going according to plan. An advance regiment had already landed successfully in northern Luzon, while three battalions had gained a foothold in southern Luzon. Homma sent another battalion to the south, and was now steaming into the Lingayen

Gulf, north of Manila, with the last three battalions. With a total of two divisions, he was preparing to assault a mountainous land defended by over ten divisions.

As the ships closed on the shoreline, the American and Filipino artillery opened up. At the same time, the weather suddenly turned worse; the clouds darkened, the wind picked up, and the waves were now towering to six feet and higher. But it was too late to turn back, and the landing craft were put in the water. Soon, the landing boats were lost to Homma's eyes in the darkness of the storm. Had they been capsized? Had they been blown up by the artillery? Were his men now dying on the beaches before heavy fire?

Suddenly, one of the transports near Homma's ship exploded in a fiery blast, the victim of an American submarine's torpedo; the ship had been carrying the hospital unit. This added to Homma's despair as he strained to see what was happening to the assault waves. The storm worsened; soon naval and air support for his troops on the beaches became impossible. "I might have been badly beaten," Homma later recalled. "The first assault wave was marooned on the beaches. If we had been counterattacked, we would have been helpless."

But Homma's men had not been counterattacked. Quite the opposite, Sugiyama's estimate of the Filipino soldier had proven surprisingly accurate. Once ashore, the Japanese had made short work of the ill-trained Philippine troops; in fact, many of the Filipinos had broken from their positions at the first sign of the Japanese and run from the battle.

The storm subsided as quickly as it had begun, and Homma received word that the immediate area had been secured. Landing operations resumed, and the remainder of the three battalions was brought to shore, Homma among them.

The invasion advanced rapidly. The northern units

were pushing down Luzon from Aparri and Vigan, while the southern force was streaking up from Legaspi to join them. At the same time, Homma's Lingayen force was fighting its way directly to the heart of the Philippines, Manila. General Wainwright retreated before Homma's advance, finally taking up positions behind the Agno river north of Manila. Everywhere, the Japanese were gaining ground rapidly; again and again, the Filipino soldiers broke from their positions and fled in terror and confusion before the smaller but more effective Japanese forces.

Within days, MacArthur's plan to defend the islands at the beaches was in shambles. Homma's forces were no longer on the beaches; they now controlled much of Luzon and were already striking for Manila itself.

Reluctantly, MacArthur abandoned the original defense plans and readopted the original War Plan Orange. His army would fight a delaying action, gradually withdrawing into the Bataan peninsula. There, and on the impregnable Corregidor, they could hold out for at least six months; by then, reinforcements from the United States would arrive and a counteroffensive would be launched.

But such a plan required two things. First, Wainwright must hold his position at the Agno river long enough to permit the withdrawal of troops from around the islands to Bataan. And second, sufficient supplies must be transferred to Bataan and Corregidor to last MacArthur's army of about 100,000 men for at least six months. Having earlier abandoned War Plan Orange, MacArthur had not stocked Bataan with supplies; this now became a critical factor.

Homma was not about to oblige MacArthur. Within a few days, his force had broken through Wainwright's position and was now advancing on a largely undefended Manila. Thousands of Philippine soldiers were tearing off their uniforms, hiding in the jungles, or just

trying to make their way back to their families; 13,000
Filipinos deserted in the withdrawal from the Agno river
alone.

Meanwhile, Homma's southern force had quickly advanced to within 140 miles of Manila. Within a few days,
the two groups would meet at the capital in a giant
pincer.

But Homma was presented with a problem. He realized
that MacArthur's plan was now to withdraw into the Bataan peninsula. From the Japanese force's present positions, he knew he might be able to cut off the retreat route
from Manila to Bataan, thus isolating MacArthur's forces
in the open and forcing a quick surrender. But this would
involve deviating from the objective of taking Manila and
heading toward Bataan instead. This would mean violating Imperial Headquarters' specific order of taking the
capital first, then dealing with the remaining forces.

Homma pondered the situation. Finally, he dispatched
only a regiment to try to slow down the withdrawal into
Bataan. With the remainder of his forces he pressed on
toward Manila.

As a result, MacArthur was able to succeed in retreating the majority of his army into the peninsula and onto
Corregidor. In doing so, he declared Manila an "open
city" (under international law a city not being used in
any way for military purpose, and so not subject to attack), thus hoping to save his adopted homeland from
further destruction. Homma, aware that the international
provisions relating to an open city were not being kept by
MacArthur, chose to ignore the declaration. As the U.S.
Army's own chief of military history later wrote, "Since
Manila was used as a base of supplies, and since a U.S.
Army headquarters was based in the city and troops
passed through it after 26 December [the date of MacArthur's declaration], it is difficult to see how Manila could
be considered an open city." Nevertheless, this was to be

the first of the many "war crimes" that Homma was later to be charged with by his conquered foe.

MacArthur retreated to Corregidor and continued directing his army from the island fortress. Wainwright remained as his commander of the forces that by now had retreated into Bataan. And Homma finally entered Manila, his principal assigned objective accomplished.

Now, Homma turned his attentions across Manila Bay to the withdrawn enemy forces. Corregidor. And Bataan.

The ensuing siege was to last for months, Homma's forces pressing down the Bataan peninsula, Wainwright's army slowly giving up ground. The mountainous terrain, jungle cover, humid heat, and disease made life miserable for both sides. But, again, it was mistakes—this time made on both sides—that finally determined the outcome and made possible the tragic finale of the Death March.

MacArthur had once again made a critical mistake in the opening days of the invasion. Reluctant to admit that his long-cherished plan of meeting the enemy at the beaches had failed miserably, he had put off executing the provisions of War Plan Orange. Most importantly, he had delayed in transferring the supplies needed for his army to Bataan. By the time supplies were being transferred, it was too late. Homma's advance had been much faster than anticipated, and the supply lines had been cut.

The most recent version of War Plan Orange had envisioned supplies on Corregidor for 10,000 men for six months; on Bataan, there were to be provisions for 43,000 men for six months. But by the time Homma had cut the supply lines, MacArthur found his army in a difficult situation. Corregidor's 10,000 men, MacArthur with them, had sufficient supplies. But on Bataan there were now not 43,000 men, but more than 80,000 soldiers and 25,000 civilian refugees. and the few supplies that had got through would supply this huge army for only *one* month.

Upon learning of this, MacArthur immediately reduced
the rations for soldiers and civilians to half the normal
amount. But the future remained grim.

MacArthur then made yet another mistake. From the
quick victories Homma had achieved, and from the chaotic reports from American and Filipino intelligence, Mac-
Arthur concluded that he was fighting a much larger force
than he actually was. Rather than two divisions, MacArthur felt that Homma was actually leading *six* divisions
against him, and he so informed Washington. This misinformation proved critical in two ways. First, Washington
felt that in view of such a large enemy force, reinforcements should not be sent: The Philippines would be written off. Second, Wainwright failed to launch a powerful
counteroffensive at Homma's numerically vastly inferior
forces, believing them to be superior. In fact, there were to
be many times in the ensuing months that Homma's depleted lines could easily have been broken by any form of
concerted attack. Instead, the American–Filipino strategy
was premised upon defense, withdrawal . . . and slow
starvation.

But General Homma was also to make a critical error.
Like MacArthur, he had incorrectly estimated the enemy
strength. Unlike MacArthur, however, Homma had *un-
derestimated* his enemy's numbers. Homma estimated enemy strength on Bataan at only 25,000—less than one-
third of the actual number; the remainder of the enemy
strength was believed to be spread throughout the Philippines, many of them disorganized after the initial fighting or deserters. And like MacArthur, Homma reported
this misinformation back to his superiors in Tokyo. The
error was to prove a critical factor in the later war-crimes
trial.

In January, Homma sent a message to MacArthur on
Corregidor.

I am well aware that you are doomed. The end is near. The question is how long you will be able to resist. You have already cut rations by half. I appreciate the fighting spirit of yourself and your troops who have been fighting with courage. Your prestige and honor have been upheld. However, in order to avoid needless bloodshed and to save the remnants of your divisions and your auxiliary troops, you are advised to surrender.

MacArthur, of course, refused. He was not the kind of man who would give in without a fight. And he believed that supplies and reinforcements would soon be on their way from the United States. On January 15th, in a message to his Philippine and American troops, MacArthur urged them not to give up because "help is on the way from the United States. Thousands of troops and hundreds of planes are being dispatched." He added to his commanders, "It is imperative that our troops hold until these reinforcements arrive. No further retreat is possible."

MacArthur could not completely be blamed for thus misleading his men. Roosevelt had wired MacArthur, urging him to fight on and saying that although he could not promise immediate aid, "every ship at our disposal is bringing to the southwest Pacific the forces which will ultimately smash the invader." On the other hand, Marshall, realizing that it would be a long time before any reinforcements of supplies could be sent to the Philippines, never held out any false hopes to MacArthur.

And so the fighting raged on, the battle line across the Bataan peninsula shifting back and forth but slowly receding as the Japanese pushed relentlessly on.

But neither were things going all that well for Homma, neither on the front nor back at Tokyo. His army had suffered many casualties, and he was faced now with the prospect of slowly fighting down a peninsula of mountainous and jungle-covered terrain, cut by swift rivers and

deep gorges. Some of his units were composed of Formo-
san troops, poorly equipped with pre–World War I weapons. And supplies were running out. One of Homma's
commanders, for example, sent an officer to the commander of a neighboring unit with the message, "Our
regiment has been out of rations for six days. I have come
to take back supplies." To this, the neighboring commander replied, "We have no food either. This morning I
gnawed half a piece of bread. All I can give is six plugs of
tobacco."

Homma tried a daring tactic. He quickly planned an
amphibious operation where troops would be landed at
two beaches behind the enemy lines. They would then
merge, thus surrounding the Filipinos and Americans.
He did not know, of course, that these units would be
landing on a peninsula swarming with over 100,000 men.
Both landing parties were wiped out.

But Homma's chief problems came not from MacArthur, but from Tokyo. At Imperial Headquarters, the
General Staff was jubilant that Manila had been taken so
swiftly. Sugiyama had been under considerable pressure
from Tojo to give him victories to boost national morale.
Now Homma had taken Manila, and Yamashita was
sweeping through Malaya toward Singapore. But gradually the realization began to sink in at the General Staff:
Manila had fallen, but so long as MacArthur remained on
Bataan and Corregidor, the valuable harbor could not be
used by the navy.

The War Cabinet now began to ask embarrassing questions. Sugiyama defended his position, saying that
Homma had failed to show the qualities of true leadership. A true commander, he argued, would have taken
Manila but also cut off the enemy from retreat and forced
a battle. Homma had run away from confronting MacArthur's troops.

In covering himself, Sugiyama caused a whispering

campaign to be started at Imperial Headquarters. As the historian Masanori Ito wrote:

> For example, one of the [staff officers] said, "Why did he let the enemy slip away to Bataan so easily?" and another, "Anyone could occupy Manila if there were no enemy defending it." The staff, who had determined the general strategy and given orders that Bataan should be ignored, had to change their attitude. But Homma and Maeda had no spare time to say, "We told you so."

Sugiyama now began to argue that Homma should be recalled. He was incompetent and afraid to fight. Nevertheless, it was decided that Homma be left in the Philippines. But his command would be cut. Since there were only 30,000 or 40,000 men on Bataan and Corregidor, as Homma had mistakenly reported, and since most of these were inferior Filipino soldiers, it was felt that Homma could accomplish the mission with fewer men than he had. MacArthur's ragged force was bottled up, and it was strictly a case of time; in any event, the troops were more needed in other areas.

General Terauchi, the commander of the Southern Army and a crony of Sugiyama and Tojo, signaled Homma that certain units were to be recalled and sent to the Dutch East Indies. Homma protested but to no avail.

Homma now tried to pull strings back in Tokyo. He informed Prince Takeda of his problems; Takeda was sympathetic and called Imperial Headquarters, urging that the units remain. Terauchi heard of this and sent an officer to Manila to ensure that his orders were carried out. Homma tried to explain his predicament to the officer, but Terauchi's representative replied that the Philippines were no longer considered a primary objective. Java was now the chief consideration. The entire Pacific campaign must be completed quickly so that troops could be transferred to the north; Russian troop movements, he explained, had been reported near the Manchukuo border.

Finally, Homma received a promise from Terauchi that a smaller unit would be sent to take the place of withdrawn units; this would be the 65th Brigade from Formosa. The 65th had only 6,500 men, drafted just the previous year and consisting predominantly of the old and physically undesirable. Homma quickly wired the unit's commander, asking him what condition the unit was in. The commanding officer, ironically a graduate of Amherst College and a close friend of President Coolidge's son, replied that the 65th was "absolutely unfit for combat duty."

Meanwhile, the heavy bombardment and artillery shelling of Corregidor continued. Most of the defenders on "The Rock" had long since withdrawn into the elaborate labyrinth of underground tunnels that honeycombed the island. The largest and most complex of these was the Malinta Tunnel, which housed MacArthur's headquarters and the majority of the 10,000-man defense force. These men would come up onto the surface in regular shifts, leaving the safety of the tunnels to take their turns at manning the huge artillery pieces with which they fired back across the bay at Homma's forces; others manned the machine gun and howitzer emplacements, ready to cut down any attempted amphibious assaults. But life on the surface was dangerous, Homma's constant barrage taking its inevitable toll.

MacArthur continued to command the Bataan campaign from his bunker in the Malinta Tunnel, calmly striding among his men with his walking stick and "field marshal's" hat, apparently oblivious to the carnage raging above him. Yet his calm and confident manner did not seem to have the desired effect on his troops fighting on Bataan. As food and supplies began running out, and morale deteriorated, the men began to grow increasingly resentful of their absentee commander. He had not left the safety of the underground tunnels for many weeks now, they noted, while they were carrying on a constant battle of attrition with the Japanese and the jungle heat. Soon, the nickname "Dugout Doug" began circulating among his troops and bitter singing was often heard:

Dugout Doug MacArthur lies
A shaking on the Rock
Safe from all the bombers
And from any sudden shock.

This widespread attitude of the American and Filipino soldiers was, of course, totally unfair. MacArthur had proven his personal courage on many occasions during his earlier career. In fact, unknown to his men, he had often ventured out of the tunnel into the shrieking nightmare of explosions on Corregidor without a helmet or any protection of any kind; on more than one occasion he was nearly killed when bombs burst near where he was standing, oblivious to his aides' pleas to take cover.

Without question, MacArthur was a courageous commander. But his men fighting and dying on Bataan had not seen him for months. Supplies were running out, and the situation seemed hopeless. Morale was at a low point, and MacArthur was the obvious source of resentment.

One of the Filipino leaders, General Aguinaldo, wrote MacArthur a message begging him to surrender; fighting on, he said, would result in thousands of lives being lost for no reason. The Philippines were lost. Why throw away lives meaninglessly?

This message was followed by a letter from President Quezon to Roosevelt, asking him to grant independence to the Philippines at once. Thus, he could announce the neutrality of his nation, and American and Japanese forces could be withdrawn.

Shaken by Aguinaldo's message and by Quezon's attitude, MacArthur reluctantly advised Roosevelt that his men were exhausted and that "complete destruction" could come at any time now. Roosevelt considered the matter, then urged MacArthur to fight on if at all possible but authorized him to negotiate a surrender if necessary.

But MacArthur was getting his second wind. He replied to Roosevelt that "I have not the slightest intention in the world of surrendering or capitulating the Filipino forces of my command." Then, with his well-known flair for the dramatic, he concluded, "I intend to fight to destruction on Bataan and then do the same on Corregidor." When it was suggested that perhaps his wife and young son should be rescued from "The Rock" by submarine, MacArthur haughtily answered that they "will stay with me to the end. We drink from the same cup. . . . I and my family will share the fate of the garrison."

But brave words were of little solace to the weakened and dying men of his command. Morale worsened, and the situation on Corregidor grew so bad that many men simply refused to leave the safety of the tunnels to take their turns on the surface. These men, derisively called "tunnel rats" by the others, began growing in numbers as supplies became depleted and living conditions worsened. Yet as bad as life was on the surface, it was little better in the dark heat of the underground tunnels, with the stench of human waste and diseased men everywhere.

But it was on Bataan that conditions were the worst. Since the rations had been cut in half at the beginning of January, supplies had steadily dwindled until by February the rations for the 80,000 soldiers and 25,000 civilians were averaging one-third of the normal amount. Rice was the principal food, but the soldiers soon turned to scouring the jungles for wild dogs, iguanas, monkeys, and snakes. Foraging for food often had tragic consequences, though: the native wild carrot, for example, was highly poisonous, and after eating them many men died in violent spasms of pain. By April, one supply officer noted, the peninsula "had been broken dry of all edible vegetation which anyone thought he could eat."

Soon, the shortage of food supplied further grounds for deterioration of morale. Many of the units in the field began to falsify their reports by doubling their estimated numbers, thereby gaining more food; one division of 7,500 men, for example, reported troop strength at 14,000. But the greatest source of anger and resentment among the troops was the unevenness of food distribution. There appeared to be little uniformity or fairness in allocation of the available food. Supply units were fed comparatively well, while front-line troops starved; influence was used by certain officers to obtain food at the expense of their soldiers; food shipments were commonly diverted from their goal by questionable means.

Looting, pilferage, and hijacking also became common on Bataan. Supply trucks moving slowly along the narrow jungle trails were easy targets for hungry men with guns. So serious did this situation become that guards were posted and instructed to shoot anyone caught looting or anyone found in a supply dump without proper authority. But the stealing continued. The guards themselves looted the food supplies, and truck drivers would throw food off to waiting friends along the road. It was a sad fact that the closer the ration trucks came to the front lines, the less they contained.

But the main source of anger to men on Bataan was Corregidor. Everyone firmly believed that MacArthur and the contingent of 10,000 men on "The Rock" were eating quite well. Unfortunately, there was much to this belief. Although life on Corregidor was not easy, it was much better than on Bataan. General Wainwright was

later to learn this when he moved to "The Rock." Used to
the starvation conditions on Bataan, he discovered Corregidor a relative land of plenty. The troops there ate
comparatively well, feeding on such luxury items as ba-
con, ham, fresh vegetables, coffee, milk, and jam—foods
which had long since disappeared from the Bataan diet.
This situation was highlighted to the troops on Bataan
one day when a truck carrying supplies to a Corregidor
unit was stopped by Bataan military police. To their surprise, the MPs found the truck stuffed with Vienna sau-
sages, raisins, lard, peas, corn, peaches, tomatoes, and
cigarettes. News of the incident spread quickly to the
front-line troops, and morale continued to deteriorate. In
a memorandum on the incident to General Beebe, the
provost marshall complained: "There is no way of preventing this sort of thing getting to the front line troops
and you can appreciate the effect on morale. The clandes-
tine manner of getting the so-called luxury items to the
Harbor Defense . . . does not seem ethical."

Lack of food was not the only problem faced by Mac-
Arthur's men. Clothing and shoes were in short supply,
and medicine was often unavailable. Tropical diseases
ran rampant in the jungles of Bataan, and few men were
not at least touched by some form of malaria, scurvy,
beriberi, vitamin deficiency, or amoebic dysentery. The
reduced food rations had so lowered the stamina of the
men that they were even being incapacitated by minor
illnesses that they had earlier been able to throw off
easily without medication. One medical officer observed
that the caloric content of the rations was "well under the
requirements for the physical work demanded, resulting
in serious loss of weight"; the absence of fats and essential vitamins, he added, was resulting in "varying de-
grees of apathy, depression, lack of aggressiveness and
irritability."

By March, the physical condition of the men on Bataan had deteriorated to critical stages. Lieutenant Colonel Harold Glattly, the senior surgeon on Bataan, estimated that at least 3,500 to 4,000 calories a day were required to maintain a soldier on Bataan; but by March the rations had been reduced to less than 1,000 calories. Lieutenant Colonel Glattly found the results of this caloric deficit "alarming in the extreme": serious muscle depletion was evident everywhere, and beriberi had become almost universal. Malnutrition, he noted, had weakened the troops to seriously vulnerable levels. Quite simply, the men were "deteriorating rapidly."

Malaria became epidemic. Mosquito netting and quinine soon ran out, and MacArthur's men were at the mercy of the disease. After inspecting the fortification on Bataan at the beginning of March, General Casey reported that the incidence of malaria was over 35 percent among front-line troops at any given time and that the disease was spreading rapidly; by the end of March, 80 percent of the men were suffering from the disease. Colonel Glattly gloomily informed General King that "a mortality rate in untreated cases of 7 to 10 percent can be expected."

As the men on Bataan became more gaunt and disease-ridden, it became increasingly difficult to identify the specific source of a particular soldier's disabling problems. Often, a man would be suffering from a combined onslaught of malaria, vitamin deficiency, amoebic dysentery, and wounds received in battle. One surgeon believed that the high malarial rate was disguising the prevailing "mental and physical exhaustion" caused by a protracted starvation diet.

Simple fatigue often proved as crippling as the rampant disease. Nerves became frayed from the constant strain of bombardment and jungle survival. Toward the end of the campaign, many of the men proved unable to

stand the nervous strain of combat any further. Men simply threw away their weapons and refused to fight.
"They were surly and physically exhausted as well as
mentally unequal to further combat duty," one medical
officer observed.

Clearly, the men on Bataan were in critical condition
and deteriorating rapidly. The average American or Filipino soldier was emaciated by starvation and further
weakened by a plethora of diseases. In many cases, he
was a walking skeleton, barely able to survive. And it
was this situation, the extent of which was not known to
the Japanese, that was to prove yet another critical factor
in the Death March.

As the American situation turned even darker, MacArthur received a message from Marshall notifying him that
Roosevelt was considering sending MacArthur to Mindanao to set up a new base of operations for the defense of
the southern Philippine Islands. At the same time, the
Australian government had forwarded a request to Roosevelt to assign MacArthur to Canberra as supreme commander of the newly formed Southwest Pacific Command. Upon receiving the request, Roosevelt instructed
MacArthur to proceed as soon as possible to Mindanao;
there, he was to shore up the defenses as best he could,
then leave for Australia.

"My first reaction," MacArthur later wrote, "was to try
and avoid the latter part of the order, even to the extent
of resigning my commission and joining the Bataan force
as a simple volunteer. But Dick Sutherland and my entire
staff would have none of it." The reluctance to leave
Corregidor was probably very real; certainly, it was in
keeping with his proven courage.

"For two days I delayed a final decision," MacArthur
recalled. "Finally, I answered the President in a message
that warned of the results that might follow the failure to

adequately sustain the Philippines. Because of the very special confidence the Filipino people and Army had in me, my sudden departure might set off a collapse of the Filipino defenses."

"Two days later," MacArthur continued, "Marshall replied, advising me that the decision as to my departure was to be left up to me. . . . For three weeks I postponed my leaving until Marshall responded with the information that the situation in Australia called for my early arrival."

There has been some speculation as to what was meant by "the decision as to my departure was to be left up to me." Was this simply a reference as to *when* MacArthur was to leave? Or had Marshall suddenly and unexpectedly bowed to MacArthur's courageous request to remain—thus putting his old antagonist on the spot? Whatever the meaning, MacArthur was afterward to insist that he left only because ordered to.

Thus, on the night of March 12 MacArthur stood on the far shores of Corregidor, prepared to depart. Standing by were four PT boats, the remains of the original force that were to have been the seed of MacArthur's coastal defense armada. But he was not to leave without a dramatic flourish. Looking about him, MacArthur later wrote,

> It was as though the dead were passing by the stench of destruction. The smell of filth thickened the night air. I raised my cap in farewell salute, and I could feel my face go white, feel a sudden, convulsive twitch in the muscles of my face. I heard someone ask, "What's his chance, Sarge, of getting through?" and the gruff reply, "Dunno. He's lucky. Maybe one in five . . ." Although the flotilla consisted of only four battle-scarred PT boats, its size was no gauge of the uniqueness of its mission. This was the desperate attempt by a commander-in-chief

and his key staff to move thousands of miles
through the enemy's lines to another war theater, to
direct a new and intensified assault.

In any event, MacArthur left Corregidor. But even the
circumstances of leaving were not to be without contro-
versy. With only four PT boats, space was severely limited; only a few badly needed military leaders could be
rescued from Corregidor's certain fate. Understandably,
MacArthur included his wife and son in this small group.
But his insensitivity—or perhaps arrogance—was shown
when he included his son's favorite Filipino "nanny" as
one of the chosen few. Again, this only served to lower
morale among the remaining troops. Defending his action, MacArthur later said, "My detractors would have
seized on any selection [of whom to take] as an opportunity for further criticism. . . . Few people outside the Ori-
ent know how completely a member of the family an
amah [nanny] can become."

Regardless of the circumstances, MacArthur was right
about the effect of his leaving upon the morale of the
Philippine people. The Filipino and American soldiers
had continued to believe that reinforcements would
eventually arrive and that they would be saved. MacArthur had promised it. But now he had suddenly left,
deserted them. Would MacArthur flee from the Philippines if supplies and troops were being sent from America? His departure was final proof that help would never
arrive.

"I came through," MacArthur said, safe in Australia,
"and I shall return." But the dramatic proclamation fell
on deaf ears in Bataan and on Corregidor. The end was
near, and the diseased and starving soldiers of MacArthur's command knew there was nothing to do but wait

for the inevitable defeat and the prison camp that would follow.

In the dark gloom of the jungles, a short song was heard:

We're the battling bastards of Bataan;
No mama, no papa, no Uncle Sam;
No aunts, no uncles, no cousins, no nieces;
No pills, no planes, no artillery pieces;
And nobody gives a damn.

4
Death March

MACARTHUR'S MEN WERE NOT THE ONLY SOLDIERS SUF-
fering from the ravages of jungle warfare. General
Homma, starting with only 43,000 soldiers, had already
lost 7,000 in combat on Bataan; another 13,000 had been
stricken with malaria, beriberi, and dysentery. While the
supply situation was better than MacArthur's, food was
nevertheless constantly in short supply, and it had become necessary to cut daily rations from sixty-two to
thirty-two ounces.

With his best units taken from him and shipped to the
East Indies, to be replaced with a smaller group of inex-
perienced and poorly equipped soldiers, Homma now
found himself in the precarious position of attempting to
dislodge a superior force firmly entrenched in terrain that
strongly favored the defenders. Much of his small army
was being used to subdue and hold other areas in Luzon,
and with battle casualties and disease taking their toll, he
was left with a pitifully small force to campaign against
Wainwright on Bataan. Had either he or MacArthur
known exactly how outnumbered the Japanese invaders

were, the battle for Bataan would probably have taken a different turn. But as it was, Homma was throwing his remaining force of about 20,000 soldiers against what he felt to be a combined American-Filipino army of about 35,000—only 25,000 of which he believed to be on Bataan. On the other side, Wainwright was leading 80,000 men on Bataan, with another 10,000 men on Corregidor; he believed, as MacArthur had told him, he was facing a superior force of about 130,000 crack Japanese troops. Neither side realized that Wainwright's vastly superior forces could have counterattacked and easily broken through the thin Japanese lines.

To Homma, and to Imperial Headquarters, it appeared that an inferior force had frustrated him in meeting his assigned objective of conquest within fifty days. January 31 had come and gone, and the enemy remained, far from beaten. Homma knew he had failed.

On February 8, Homma called a conference of all subordinate commanders to discuss proposed new strategies. By nine o'clock in the morning all the officers were present. All but Homma. After waiting for a period of time, the operations chief, Colonel Nakayama, went over to his general's office. There, seated at the desk, was General Homma, tears streaming down his face. A message was lying on the desk next to him. It was from Imperial Headquarters. "The Emperor is very concerned about your strategic situation. Why are you making no progress?"

Nakayama was shocked. To be criticized by the emperor was the most humiliating thing imaginable; it almost demanded that Homma take the only honorable course and commit *seppuku*.

But Homma was crying not out of self-pity but from rage. He knew that the cable had been sent by Sugiyama, using the emperor's name. Sugiyama, who had ordered him to ignore MacArthur's retreat to Bataan and who had then decimated his command by withdrawing his best

units to Java. And now this man was publicly blaming
Homma for the failure.

Drying his eyes now, slowly bringing himself under
control, Homma walked with Nakayama to the meeting
room. He listened to the views of his men on what
course to take. Nakayama reminded them that their objective remained to destroy the enemy on Bataan. Maeda,
however, pointed out that their forces were simply not
strong enough; the attack should be discontinued, the
rest of the Philippines occupied, and the enemy on Bataan blockaded until they finally surrendered when supplies ran out. Homma listened to the views of the two
men, then pondered the situation. The *bushido* code was
deeply ingrained in him, and it dictated that he keep
attacking until the last Japanese soldier lay dead. Yet
Homma somehow could not bring himself to throw his
men's lives away senselessly.

Finally, Homma made his decision. He dictated a letter to Maeda, to be forwarded by him to Imperial
Headquarters:

> As reported to you previously, the enemy has taken
> up a defensive line from Bagac to Orion through the
> northern foothills of Mount Samat. At the expense
> of great labors he has built defensive positions deep
> in the jungle. . . . They have ample ammunition and
> can bring down accurate fire on us by day and by
> night. The enemy can use jeeps, armored cars, and
> tanks along the tracks he has constructed in the
> Mount Samat area; he can use his knowledge of the
> terrain and take advantage of our poor communica-
> tions. He has considerable mobility. Also he com-
> mands the sea from the mouth of Manila Bay to the
> western coast of Bataan. . . . Our present situation is
> that we see no prospect of success and are in a seri-
> ous state. If we try to go on with the operation,
> things will become even worse. We urge you to con-
> sider just how necessary it is to capture [Bataan] and

whether the expenditure in effort and casualties would prove worthwhile. We consider that our first duty should be to administer the Philippines and extract all possible resources from it."

When Sugiyama read this message, he burst into a fit of rage. Immediately, he called a meeting of the General Staff and recommended that Homma should be relieved of command as soon as possible. But this was a delicate proposal. Theoretically, every commander of a division or larger unit was considered to be appointed as such by the emperor himself; removal of Homma could be interpreted as a criticism of the sovereign. Not only that, one of the generals pointed out to Sugiyama, recalling Homma would be a public admission of failure. How could the General Staff remove Homma after his quick capture of Manila had been hailed all over Japan as a great victory? It could prove a serious blow to public morale and an embarrassment to Tojo's government.

In the end, Sugiyama agreed to a compromise: Homma would remain, but his chief of staff, General Maeda, would be recalled. In his place, Sugiyama would appoint a much more aggressive man, Major General Takaji Wachi. Sugiyama would then control Homma's chief of staff. But to increase this control over Homma, he also arranged for the appointment to Homma's staff of another "aggressive" Sugiyama crony, the infamous Colonel Masanobu Tsuji. And it was this that was to be the final nail in the coffin of those soon to take part in the Death March.

Colonel Tsuji was a man widely known throughout the Japanese Army—and universally detested. He was a strange, almost mystical figure, who constantly declared to all those around him that he was divinely immune from death. He claimed to have mystical sources of power and apparently had ready access to both Sugiyama and Tojo. He had a reputation of cruelty and barbarous

conduct toward the enemy and had repeatedly caused
atrocities in China and Malaya by giving heinous orders
in the names of other officers without the slightest permission. He had already been instrumental in the mass
murders of 5,000 Chinese nationals. Tsuji was generally
regarded as a government spy; wherever he was assigned, his fellow officers knew that they were under
scrutiny.

And so Homma's personal staff, charged with advising
him and carrying out his directives, became infiltrated
and, in fact, indirectly controlled by Sugiyama.

But the letter was not a total loss. Grudgingly, headquarters agreed to send Homma the reinforcements he
needed. By mid-March, Lieutenant General Kitamura
had arrived from China with the 4th Division, and Major
General Nagano followed with the 21st Division; soon
after that, the 1st Artillery Corps arrived and then a contingent of planes.

Homma's first reaction upon reviewing the troops,
which had now more than doubled his strength, was one
of horror. The 4th Division was a unit filled with misfits,
grown soft on occupation duty in China. "This division
must be the worst equipped in the entire Japanese Army," Homma muttered to an aide. Was Sugiyama again
trying to sabotage Homma's efforts?

Angrily, he wrote Imperial Headquarters, demanding
weapons, supplies, and uniforms to bring the 4th Division up to minimal standards. This request was ignored,
but two heavy bomber regiments were transferred to his
command.

Homma prepared for the assault on Bataan. He was
unhappy with the condition of his forces, but as he wrote
in his diary:

> I think it is true that while we are in a state of suffer-
> ing, the enemy is in a worse condition. When they

were in a bad position and their attacks at a stand-
still, General MacArthur sent a report about 9th February to the United States saying that the darkest
stage has come since Pearl Harbor, and on the 10th
another message saying that the battle of Bataan is
hopeless. Furthermore, the War Department said
the chances of holding their positions were very
slim. When battle conditions do not progress I
should always remind myself of this kind of thing.

He then turned to an analysis of the enemy's forces,
vastly underrating their numbers but overrating their
condition.

The maximum enemy strength [throughout the
Philippines] is 50,000 men. Exluding personnel on
Corregidor, garrisons on other islands, guards on the
shores from east to west Bataan, the enemy has approximately 20,000 infantrymen. If 25,000 men were
lined up over a distance of 25 kilometers [across the
peninsula], each man would be one meter apart.
Such a line should be very easy to penetrate.

It seems that the enemy has about the same
amount of training as our men, and junior officers
who have been trained at universities. They may be
very efficient in battle. Filipino officers who have
devoted their lives to America have great fighting
spirit. It would appear that they are never allowed
to go hungry. The enemy has a tendency to fire its
guns wildly but seems to have ample stocks of
ammunition.

On March 28, Homma called together his staff and
issued final instructions. The 65th Brigade would carry
on the main attack, with the 16th Division carrying out
diversionary attacks to the west. The 21st Division would
be held in reserve. The attack would be supported by
heavy artillery barrages and air bombardment.

On April 3, the artillery and bombers began. For two

days, Wainwright's front lines were shelled and bombed. Then, the Filipino 41st Division began to fall apart, and General Nara quickly advanced through the breach with the 65th Brigade. Homma then brought up his tanks, and Wainwright's 21st Division fell back in retreat. Soon, units all along the line were buckling and falling back in confused retreat.

By April 7, the offensive was a spectacular success. Wainwright's forces had retreated halfway down the peninsula and were largely disorganized. An order went out from General King's headquarters for his soldiers to destroy all artillery, ammunition, weapons, and tanks.

On the following morning, Colonel Everett Williams and Major Marshall Hurt appeared under a flag of truce to arrange a surrender meeting between King and Homma. They were instructed to return with their commander. Homma sent Colonel Nakayama to represent him at the meeting; General King appeared as commander of the American-Filipino forces. Nakayama assumed that King was Wainwright; King, on the other hand, assumed Nakayama was Homma. When the confusion was straightened out, Nakayama accepted King's surrender reluctantly. He had assumed that this was Wainwright, surrendering all forces in the Philippines and was not happy at accepting only a partial surrender.

Homma experienced a vast sense of relief at the fall of Bataan. He expected no congratulations from Imperial Headquarters and received none. He now turned all of his attention to planning and directing the assault on Corregidor. The care and transport of the prisoners on Bataan was delegated to subordinates.

General Wainwright was now commanding all forces on the Philippine Islands from Corregidor, where he had fled from Bataan. He knew his position on Corregidor was desperate, but he had his orders from MacArthur to hold until relieved by reinforcements. Nevertheless, as conditions steadily worsened, Wainwright signaled Mac-Arthur for further orders.

MacArthur radioed back that he was "utterly opposed under any circumstances or conditions to the ultimate capitulation of this command" and that Wainwright should "prepare and execute an attack upon the enemy" once food and supplies were exhausted. The idea of such a suicidal attack was, of course, ridiculous. But Wainwright remained silent and continued to withstand the constant barrages from Homma's guns and planes.

The men on Corregidor knew their days were numbered, of course. Bataan had fallen, and reinforcements would not be coming. With the Japanese artillery aimed down their throats, they could have had no illusions about the future. All they could do was prepare for the inevitable attack with the determination to make it as costly as possible to the enemy.

But the invasion was not to come immediately. Across the bay, Homma stared at the fortified island with mixed feelings. He admired Wainwright's courage, but he felt an impotent rage. Now, when victory was so close, and with sufficient troops to accomplish the task, a malaria epidemic had spread through southern Bataan, decimating his forces. His men lay stricken now by the thousands, with quinine nowhere to be had. He had radioed Tokyo for the precious medicine, but it was to be many days before his units were at sufficient strength to attempt an amphibious assault on the cannon-studded fortress. Meanwhile, Homma could only stare at the island in frustration and go over his plans once again.

Finally, on May 1st the operation began. At six o'clock in the morning Homma's heavy artillery increased their fire, and the heavy bombers began dropping their loads in wave after wave. The surface of Corregidor was being turned into a no-man's land, yet almost miraculously Wainwright's cannon continued to return the fire. "Situation here is fast becoming desperate," Wainwright signaled MacArthur. "With artillery that outranges anything we have except two guns, he [Homma] keeps up a terrific bombardment as well as aerial bombing."

The ability of the Corregidor garrison to withstand a Japanese assault after the heavy shelling was doubtful. In the previous three weeks, there had been over six hundred casualties, and those on "The Rock" who had not escaped injury were in poor physical condition. Most of the coastal guns had been destroyed, and the sand-bagged machine-gun positions had been battered beyond use. Wainwright informed General Marshall in response to a request for his frank opinion, "I estimate that we have something less than an even chance to beat off an assault."

The final day of pre-assault bombardment took place on May 5. "There was a steady roar from Bataan," one officer later recalled, "and a mightier volume on Corregidor. A continuous pall of dust and debris hung over everything. There was a feeling of doom mingled with wonder . . ."

Then, late in the afternoon, the barrage slowly eased. "It took no mental giant," Wainwright later recalled, "to figure out . . . that the enemy was ready to come against Corregidor."

The men waited in their emplacements for the coming assault. All around them, the island lay "scorched, gaunt, and leafless, covered with the chocolate dust of countless explosions and pitted with shellholes." They were living almost on nerve alone now. The men had only enough water to last for four more days. There was a limit to human endurance and that limit, Wainwright told Marshall, "has long since been passed."

At ten o'clock at night, two hours before the moon was

to come out, Homma dispatched units of the 4th Division across Manila Bay in landing boats. But the invasion miscarried almost immediately. Unknown to Homma, the westward tide along Manila's shore shifted to an eastward tide near Corregidor. The landing craft began drifting apart, most of them heading for the wrong part of the island. Floating directly under the guns of the fortress, they were caught broadside and blown out of the water one after another. Only one-third of the assault force survided to reach the island.

On Bataan, Homma strained to see across the bay. But he could only make out the orange bursts of Wainwright's cannons and the smaller flashes of small-arms fire. Then he received word that the leading assault waves had been wiped out. "My God!" he exclaimed. "I have failed miserably."

Then he received further word: Some of the forces had survived and were now conducting an assault from the beach. Homma had 14,000 troops standing by, but there were fewer than twenty landing boats available: the success of the operation rested with the survivors now on the island. If Wainwright counterattacked against the surviving assault forces, they would be decimated.

Unknown to Homma, however, Colonel Sato was rallying the remainder of his forces on the beaches behind three tanks which had made it to shore. Fighting raged on through the night, but the three tanks proved the deciding edge. By early next morning, a small band of 300 Japanese soldiers—all that was left of the Japanese force—stood near the entrance to Malinta Tunnel, the three tanks next to them.

Inside the tunnel with the shattered remains of his command, sick and wounded men lying all around him, Wainwright agonized over his decision. MacArthur had been clear—no surrender is possible. Yet he knew that if he did not surrender, a massacre would ensue. Finally,

Wainwright authorized General Beebe to radio an offer of surrender to the Japanese. The campaign in the Philippines was about to end at last.

Homma sent Colonel Nakayama to meeet with Wainwright. Wainwright, however, insisted on dealing with Homma personally. Within hours, the two men met at a village on Bataan. Wainwright offered Homma a formal note of surrender of forces on Corregidor. But Homma insisted that he would accept no partial surrender: Wainwright must surrender all forces in the Philippines or none. Then Wainwright, reluctant to give up additional forces—particularly those of General Sharp in the southern part of the Philippines—lied to Homma, telling him that he commanded only the Corregidor garrison. Unknown to Wainwright, however, Homma had intercepted an earlier message from General King acknowledging Wainwright's position as commander of all American-Filipino forces.

Homma now became angry. To him, the conduct of war was a gentleman's work, and Wainwright was lying to him, taking him for a fool and attempting to avoid an honorable leader's responsibilities. Again, Wainwright was caught in the agonizing conflict of decision. Sharp's forces to the south were still capable of resistance. Yet the price on Corregidor would be high if he refused to capitulate. Finally, Wainwright consulted with his staff, then turned to Homma and said, "I am willing to surrender the entire Philippine garrison."

Still angry, Homma replied, "How can you make this offer, since you have already denied your authority to make it? I advise you to return to Corregidor and think the matter over. If you see fit to surrender, then surrender to the commanding officer of our forces on Corregidor." With this, Homma walked out of the room.

Later, Wainwright signaled the commanding officer and tendered his surrender. Reluctantly, he radioed Gen-

I

Credits for pictures on the following seven pages, covering the background and trial of General Masaharu Homma:

Page II

Top left: captured Japanese war picture of Homma and aides during an inspection tour, August 1944 *(US Army Photograph)*

Top right: captured Japanese war picture of captured U.S. troops following the fall of Bataan *(US Army Photograph)*

Bottom: Homma disembarks on Philippine soil *(captured war photo, National Archives)*

Page III

Top: U.S. troops during the "Death March" *(captured war photo, National Archives)*

Bottom left: the Death March *(captured war photo, National Archives)*

Bottom right: aerial view of Corregidor Island *(National Archives)*

Page IV

Top: captured Japanese war picture of U.S. soldiers and sailors surrendering to Japanese forces at Corregidor Island *(US Army Photograph)*

Bottom: captured Japanese war picture of General Homma discussing surrender terms with General Wainwright *(US Army Photograph)*

Page V

Top: members of the military commission at the Homma war crimes trial *(US Army Photograph; Photographer: Gosfield)*

Bottom: Homma defense counsel from left to right: *(seated)* Capt. George Ott, Lt. Leonard Nataupsky, Maj. John H. Skeen, Jr., Homma, Capt. Frank Coper; *(standing)* Lt. Haig Kantaria, Capt. George A. Furness, Lt. Robert L. Pelz, Lt. Robert Polski *(US Army Photograph; Photographer: Berry)*

Page VI

Top: General Homma takes the stand in his own defense, February 6, 1946 *(US Army Photograph; Photographer: Trudeau)*

Bottom: General Homma and Fujiko Homma talk during a recess period outside the High Commissioner's residence in Manila, where the trial was held *(US Army Photograph; Photographer: John Kuchyna)*

Page VII

Top: Fujiko Homma testifies, February 7, 1946 *(US Army Photograph: Photographer: John Kuchyna)*

Bottom: General Homma sobs while his wife testifies in his defense, February 7, 1946 *(US Army Photograph: Photographer: John Kuchyna)*

Page VIII

Top: Homma appears deeply dejected over the testimony of Mrs. Luz Villaluna de Santos (not seen), who relates the story of the brutalities at Fort Santiago Prison, where her husband was confined before his execution, January 7, 1946 *(US Army Photograph: Photographer: Trudeau)*

Bottom: Homma awaiting transfer to Omori Prison in Japan after his arrest *(US Army Photograph: Photographer: Pierce)*

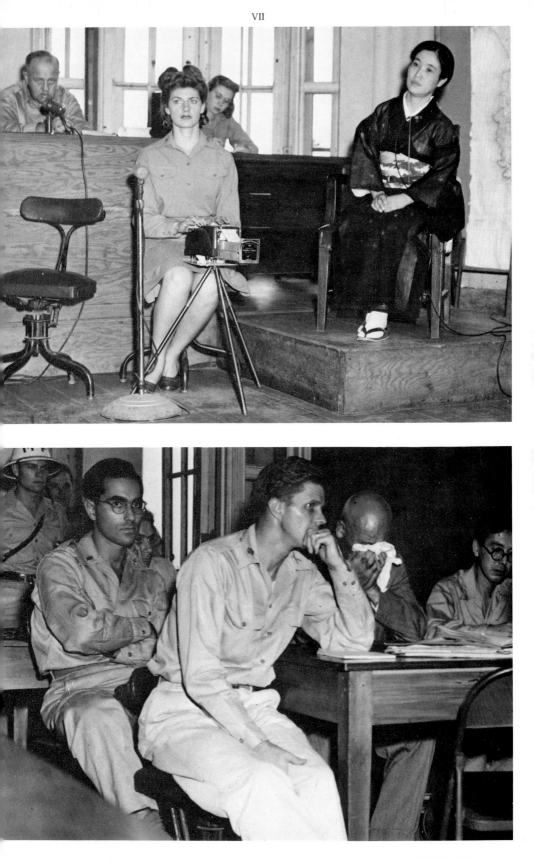

eral Sharp to give up his Visayan-Mindanao Force in the south.

Sharp immediately radioed to MacArthur, repeating Wainwright's orders which were in direct opposition to the standing orders MacArthur had left to fight to the last. Enraged when he heard of Wainwright's surrender, MacArthur replied to Sharp: "Orders emanating from General Wainwright have no validity. If possible, separate your force into small elements and initiate guerrilla operations." At the same time, he contacted Marshall in Washington and informed him that "I believe Wainwright has temporarily become unbalanced, and his condition renders him susceptible of enemy use."

This was, of course, totally unfair. Wainwright had valiantly struggled throughout the Bataan campaign, then defended a hopeless position on Corregidor. His men had undergone terrible hardships, and Wainwright himself had suffered heavily from disease and the constant strain of combat. Yet when MacArthur was later awarded the Medal of Honor for his part in the Bataan campaign, he rejected Marshall's suggestion that Wainwright—then in a POW camp—be granted the same honor. Wainwright simply did not deserve it, MacArthur said.

"If Bataan was to be destroyed," MacArthur wrote later from the safety of Australia, "it should have been on the field of battle in order to extract the full toll from the enemy. To this end, I had long ago prepared a comprehensive plan for cutting a way out if food and ammunition failed. . . . I told [Marshall] I would be very glad to rejoin the command temporarily and take charge of this movement. But Washington failed to approve. Had it done so, the dreadful "Death March" which followed the surrender . . . would never have taken place . . . . "

After Bataan had been captured, Homma had turned to organizing a compaign against Corregidor. Such a cam-

paign would, of course, have to be launched from the
southern end of the Bataan peninsula. But before operations could begin, the peninsula would have to be cleared
of all American and Filipino soldiers, thousands of whom
were straggling in from the jungles every day to surrender. As a proficient commander, Homma had foreseen the necessity for clearing out prisoners once Bataan
had been conquered and for transporting them to prisoner-of-war camps. What he had not foreseen, however,
was that the American-Filipino forces on Bataan numbered not the approximately 25,000 he expected but over
100,000—and most of them suffering from disease and
starvation.

Like any good leader, Homma had arranged for the
logistics of prisoner care and transportation long before
the actual surrender, and he had assigned five senior
officers to work out the task. The 14th Division's transport officer would supply trucks for the transportation to
the camps, Major Hisashi Sekiguchi of the Medical Corps
would arrange for medical treatment for the prisoners,
and Major Moriya Wada, a supply officer, was in charge
of providing proper food and clothing. Colonel Toshi-
mitsu Takatsu was assigned to administering the operation, and Major General Yoshikate Kawane was given
overall command.

On March 23, ten days before Homma launched his
final campaign against Bataan, these five men submitted
their plan to him for approval. There were two phases to
the plan. The first, to be directed by Colonel Takatsu,
involved gathering the captured soldiers and staging
them for removal to Camp O'Donnell in central Luzon,
approximately ninety miles away. This involved marching the roughly 25,000 men from southern Bataan to the
staging area at Balanga, a distance of nineteen miles. As
nineteen miles was considered an easy day's march for a
Japanese soldier, the plan assumed the Americans and

Filipinos would need no transportation. Nor would food be necessary on the first day, as the prisoners could use their own rations on the march. Neither Homma nor his staff could realize the pitiful condition in which they were to find the enemy soldiers; they could not know that these prisoners would not have even the one day's rations envisioned by the plan.

Phase two would be directed by Major General Kawane himself. This would involve the transportation of the prisoners from the staging area at Balanga to Camp O'Donnell. Two hundred transport trucks had been allotted to ferry the 25,000 men over a stretch of thirty-three miles to San Fernando; from there, waiting freight trains would carry them north thirty miles to Capas. Finally, the men would march the last eight miles to Camp O'Donnell.

Kawane explained to Homma that field hospitals would be set up at Balanga and San Fernando to care for the sick and wounded, and smaller field units would be established along the route. There would be periodic rest areas every few miles, offering water and rest facilities.

Satisfied that the plan conformed to the Geneva Convention articles relating to the treatment of prisoners of war, Homma instructed Major Wada to draft the order for its execution. In that order, Homma specifically directed that all prisoners were to be treated "in a friendly spirit."

Homma now turned all of his attentions to the direction of his campaign against Wainwright on Corregidor. He was satisfied that Kawane's plan was a good one, and he had confidence that his staff would supervise its execution satisfactorily.

In the chaotic confusion that followed the surrender on Bataan, Homma had no time to talk with captives or oversee the care and transport of prisoners. Corregidor demanded his full attention. In fact, all available records indicate that Homma actually met only one captured enemy on Bataan. A staff officer with General King, Colonel Collier, had been considered of interest and was taken to Homma shortly after the surrender. Collier later recalled talking with Homma in a mango grove, about a mile north of where King had just tendered his surrender. He remembered sitting in folding metal chairs at a table set up in the grove and carrying on an easy conversation with the Japanese general without the help of an interpreter. Homma had asked him a few questions in a relaxed and friendly manner, mostly about what the fighting had been like on the American side. Then he commented that he expected to capture Corregidor in about a week. When Collier asked him if it would be possible to join General King, Homma answered, "Certainly," and immediately wrote out a pass and signed it. He smiled at Collier and said, "Your worries are over." Rising to shake his hand in farewell, Homma added, "Japan treats her prisoners well. You may even see my country in cherry-blossom time and that is a beautiful sight."

The prisoner of war plans began to fall apart right from the beginning. Slowly, as the thousands of bedraggled Americans and Filipiinos continued streaming out of the jungles in seemingly unending numbers, it began to dawn on Kawane and the others—there were more than 25,000 prisoners. Many more. And they were in much worse condition than ever imagined. Many of the prisoners resembled living skeletons; nearly all of them were malnutritioned and suffering from either malaria or dysentery or both. Where medical officer Sekiguchi had estimated a 10 to 20 percent disease rate, there was 80 to 90; where Kawane and Takatsu had estimated a total of 25,000 men, there were 100,000. Few of the Americans or Filipinos had the assumed rations for the first day, and few were in any condition to make what would normally be a routine march for an infantryman.

Quite simply, Kawane's plans could not cope with a human wave of tens of thousands of sick and starving men. Homma's own soldiers had had their rations reduced by half because of lack of food, and medical supplies were chronically in short supply. Yet Kawane was now being overwhelmed with a captured army more than twice the size Homma's entire army had ever been—a captured army of diseased, starving, wounded, and dying men.

Kawane and his fellow officers tried to cope with the massive problems as best they could, but the situation was hopeless. There was not nearly enough food, not enough medicine, not enough clothing. The transportation system broke down immediately. Two hundred trucks could not transport 100,000 men. Yet the men could not be left at the staging area; there was only enough food there to feed 25,000 men the short time it was to take to move them out to San Fernando. There was no choice—the Americans and Filipinos were rounded up and ordered to begin walking. And so the Death March began.

Just as quickly as the transportation system broke down, so did the medical and supply facilities along the route become smothered in a sea of human suffering. Medical officers, corpsmen, cooks, quartermasters—none were prepared for the living tidal wave that hit them. Yet most of the Japanese assigned to the operation did what they could. And the result was predictable. As all reports from Americans and Filipinos later indicated, there was a dramatic contrast in the treatment received by prisoners in different locations. While one man would ride in a truck in comfort to Camp O'Donnell without incident, another would collapse on a dirt road and die of thirst under the blistering jungle sun. While one man would receive medical treatment, eat well, and be handed cigarettes by smiling Japanese soldiers, another one mile behind him would be viciously beaten to the ground and then bayoneted. There was no sense to any of it. In the chaotic conditions that prevailed, the treatment a given prisoner received was purely a matter of random chance.

And the men began dying. Strung out along the dirt roads from Bataan to Camp O'Donnell in a long, unending line of slowly moving humanity, the men began dying. By the hundreds they died. Men died from exhaustion. Men starved to death. Men fell to the ground, rotting away from disease. And men were brutally murdered by Japanese soldiers.

To understand how the atrocities could have taken place, despite Homma's specific directive, it is necessary to understand three factors. First, most of the Japanese soldiers had suffered through the Bataan campaign, many with painful wounds and disease. Friends had been lost to American and Filipino guns. Many of these soldiers, then, were in a vengeful mood, ready to take out their months of frustration on the nearest enemy; it was only their officers that held them in check. Moreover, the Japanese mind must be understood: Under the *Bushido* code, a soldier fought to the death—he never surrendered; to be captured was a great dishonor and demanded *seppuku* at the earliest opportunity. These Americans and Filipinos, then, were objects of contempt to many Japanese soldiers, violators of a soldier's code of honor.

The second problem was the scarcity of supervision. There were simply not enough Japanese officers to control all phases of the operation adequately. Where one officer may be sufficient to command one hundred enlisted men under normal circumstances, this structure broke down when the one hundred men were spread out as guards over a mile-long line of prisoners. One officer could not adequately supervise his men over such a distance, and there were many miles of prisoners: any one given Japanese soldier could be alone without his commanding officer for hours or even days. The opportunities to take out his pent-up hatred and rage were not rare.

The third factor that contributed directly to the infamous atrocities of the Death March was that some of the officers themselves were engaged in a vendetta against the hated enemy prisoner. Much of this has now been attributed to the infamous Colonel Tsuji. Tsuji had been very busy since his arrival in Manila. Unknown to Homma, he had convinced several of Homma's field officers that the Philippine campaign was a racial war and that all prisoners should be executed. Then after the surrender on Bataan, he had resorted to his old trick of giving orders in other officers' names.

Colonel Takeo Imai, one of Homma's most trusted commanders in the field, remembers receiving a call from a "mysterious" officer who identified himself as a division staff officer. The officer ordered Imai to "kill all prisoners and those offering to surrender." Imai refused, but the officer insisted the order was from Imperial Headquarters in Tokyo. Imai again refused and hung up the field phone. Infuriated at this violation of the *samurai* code, Imai ordered his staff to free all the prisoners and give them directions on the best way to escape from Bataan. More than a thousand Americans and Filipinos were thus set free into the jungles, heading north. Imai watched them go, commenting to one of his aides that no Japanese officer would have issued an order to murder prisoners.

A similar order was relayed by the mysterious officer on the staff-headquarters line to Major General Ikuta. But like Imai, Ikuta refused to believe such an order would come from a Japanese general. It is unknown how many obeyed the "order." What is known is that to his death Homma remained ignorant of Tsuji's orders.

And so the Death March wound on to its grisly conclusion. Somewhere between eighty and one-hundred thousand men left Bataan for the prisoner-of-war camps. Approximately seven thousand of them never made it. Their emaciated bodies, many with bayonet wounds or heads neatly severed from the necks, lay strewn along the eighty-mile-long path of infamy.

It was not until three years later that Homma learned of the deaths of seven thousand prisoners. He had been totally absorbed in the conduct of the campaign against Wainwright's stronghold on Corregidor. Tokyo was demanding control of the valuable Manila Bay, and he was already far behind schedule. And it took him almost a month to take "The Rock," a month during which the Death March had taken place. It is not surprising that he had forgotten about the prisoner operation, content that it was being taken care of satisfactorily by Kawane. And it is not surprising that Kawane decided against bothering Homma with his problems. Under the soldier's code, Kawane knew the problem was his to solve; Homma was concentrating on more pressing matters. And even Kawane was unaware of the atrocities being committed by individual soldiers or of Tsuji's campaign of death.

Yet Homma was later to be charged by MacArthur with having personally committed war crimes. Although it was never alleged that Homma ordered any of the mistreatment or atrocities, or that he had even been *aware* of their existence, he was nevertheless held to stand trial for his life. It was enough that he was technically in command when the acts took place.

Nor were the enumerated crimes limited to the Death March. Homma was also to be charged personally with mistreatment in the prison camps. Again, Homma had delegated the supervision of the camps to subordinates—

as is the practice in any army. And, again, the overwhelming numbers of prisoners and lack of adequate supervision of guards resulted in isolated instances of brutality. But the dates exonerate Homma here too. He had
received the surrender of Corregidor on May 8 and was
later to be relieved of command and sent back to Japan
on June 9. During that thirty days, Homma had to "mop-
up" in skirmishes around the Philippines, engage in
countering guerrilla operations, arrange for the surrender
of General Sharp's command, occupy the Philippines, establish an administration to govern the country, deal
with Tokyo, and handle literally hundreds of other matters. While hindsight is a wonderful thing, it would have
been unrealistic to have expected Homma personally to
supervise the prisoner-of-war camps during this busy
one-month period.

Without question, Homma knew nothing about any of
the atrocities with which he was to be charged. MacArthur's prosecutor would not even contend that he had.
But he should have known, it would later be said. In the
quiet, logical, orderly, antiseptic world of the courtroom,
far removed from the violence of battle and pressures of
command, it would be said that Homma had been negligent. And that he must pay with his life.

Colonel Tsuji continued to be a busy man. He had
sewn the seeds of race war in some of Homma's field
officers, and he had directed the killing of prisoners on
the march and later in camps. Now he conspired to destroy Homma himself.

"Homma lacks ability," he secretly signaled back to
Sugiyama. "His staff is dull and stupid." Then he told
Sugiyama that Homma had been defying Sugiyama's
specific orders. Sugiyama had directed Homma to distrib-
ute propaganda to the Filipinos to the effect that the

Americans had mistreated them. Homma had refused to
do this, Tsuji correctly reported, and had even said that
the Americans had been excellent administrators, and it
was up to him to prove to the Philippine people that the
Japanese could be even better ones.

Sugiyama brought the matter before the General Staff.
Homma was disobedient. He was incompetent; he failed
miserably in the Philippines, requiring the help of units
needed badly elsewhere. And he was disloyal. Did the
General Staff have to be reminded of Homma's known
sympathies? Sugiyama asked. He had been the leader of
the small pro-Anglo faction; he had opposed Tojo, opposed war, and even opposed the General Staff's strategy
for the Philippines. And his Western leanings had been
reflected in the field: All reports, Sugiyama said, indicated that Homma had been "too soft" on the Americans
and Filipinos.

On June 9, 1942, Homma was relieved of his command
and brought home in disgrace. He was placed in a mean-
ingless reserve unit, the commander of a group of old
men. He was never again during the war to leave Japan.

But Homma left the Philippines without regret. He
longed to be with his wife again, he told his men. Whatever criticisms the General Staff had of his conduct, he
expressed confidence that he had done his duty. When
asked by the writer Hidemi Kon what he thought of Mac-
Arthur now that he was leaving, Homma replied, "I
think of him as a good soldier and a good political admin-
istrator. I am quite satisfied to have fought against him
for my honor."

As events were to show, MacArthur did not share
Homma's gracious attitude. MacArthur had been defeated in battle for the first time in his life—and by a
vastly inferior force. He would not forget.

Book Two: Manila

5
The Tiger of Malaya

TOMOYUKI YAMASHITA WAS BORN ON NOVEMBER 8, 1885, in a small village in Shikoku, located along a river in the rugged mountains that run through the center of Japan. His father was a simple country doctor, content to make his rounds in the quiet isolation of the backwoods district and let his youngest son spend his youth playing in the hills and fields of the mountains he loved so much.

Of this early, formative period, one of Yamashita's closest friends later wrote:

> The child is the father of the man, and the place of birth and early childhood had much to do with the formation of the personality and character of the future general. Nestled in the quiet isolation of this mountainous district, cut off as it was from the hustle and bustle of modern civilization, the boy Tomoyuki grew up to be a natural, healthy, peace-loving youth—clean-cut, open, upright, industrious,

103

and straightforward, qualities which form the foundation of his character today. The surrounding hills were covered with thick, verdant foliage, traversed by countless clear, sparkling streams and rivulets. The villagers were naive, kindhearted, and contented people, free from the cunning and scheming of their worldly-wise and money-ambitious city brothers. It was in this environment of natural beauty and harmony, in the midst of peace and contentment, that Tomoyuki spent his most formative years. As a boy, he was carefree, healthy, and mentally as well as physically alert. He was fond of spending his time out in the open, roaming the hills and fields he loved best, which caused some concern to his parents and teachers.

His love for nature caused more than a little concern. Yamashita's mother, a very gentle and affectionate woman, could not bring herself to tear her youngest son away from the happiness he found in the mountains. Yet his grades at the village elementary school were poor and getting no better. It was his father's hope that he would follow him in the medical profession, as Tomoyuki's older brother was studying hard to do. But his grades, if not corrected, would prevent this.

It fell upon the grandmother to discipline the youngest Yamashita. She would periodically talk to him in her room, sternly chastising him for selfishly thinking of no one but himself. At last, Tomoyuki's grades improved— but only enough to pass the courses and graduate from elementary school.

The situation changed, however, when Yamashita was forced to leave his home in the mountains to attend high school in the city some thirty miles away. Isolated now from his beloved trees and rivers and animals, his academic record improved dramatically. At the end of the first year, he returned home proudly wearing a medal indicating an award of scholarship, to be welcomed by his greatly relieved mother and grandmother.

It was now time to decide what career the young Yamashita would follow. His older brother was already beginning his medical career, following in their father's footsteps, and both of his sisters had married doctors. Yet he soon found himself enrolled in the Hiroshima District Military Preparatory School, training to become an army officer. Asked why this radical deviation in career selection, General Yamashita later reflected: "It was perhaps my destiny. I did not choose this career. My father suggested the idea perhaps because I was big and healthy, and my mother did not seriously object because she believed, bless her soul, that I would never pass the highly competitive entrance examination."

Yamashita soon took and passed the examination at Hiroshima and was sent to the Cadet's Academy, Japan's equivalent of West Point. Oddly enough, Yamashita excelled in every aspect of his military education. His grades were exemplary, and, like Homma, he was eventually to be graduated with high honors. But it was his character and leadership that set him apart at the military academy. "In school," a fellow officer later recalled, "he was both popular and respected by his classmates because of his simplicity, kindheartedness, and industry. He never strove for leadership, nor was he ever a member of any faction or clique. He was always the mediator in the usual arguments that boys always got into. Even the hot-headed among his classmates respected the calm, open-minded fairness of the country-bred youth and abided by his fair, impartial judgment."

He had grown from a healthy, robust country boy into a heavily muscled bear of a man. Like Homma, he was large for a Japanese. And like Homma, it was his massive build that gave him his powerful appearance, a thick-set body that seemed at first to be fat but on closer look was gristle layered with muscle. The stocky body rose straight up from fireplug thighs to broad shoulders which seemed to merge directly into his bullet-shaped head; no visible neck supported the round, calmly passive face. Undoubtedly, his bulldog appearance helped mask the gentle soul within the military uniform.

Upon graduation in 1908, Yamashita was commissioned a second lieutenant in the infantry. He quickly established himself as a hard-working officer and gifted leader, popular with both his men and his superiors. Within three years, he was named to the staff of the infantry school and in 1914 was appointed to the prestigious army staff college. In 1917 he joined the army General Staff; after two years with the General Staff, Yamashita was transferred to the War Ministry, where he was to remain for the next eighteen years, with occasional special assignments to Europe and the United States.

It was at this point in his military career that young Yamashita first became embroiled in the internal politics of the Imperial Army. And, as with General Homma, it was this that was largely to determine his fate—ending eventually in a courtroom in Manila.

Within the Imperial Army ruling strata, there were two different schools of thought on the ultimate responsibility of the military—that of the General Staff and that of the War Ministry. Those officers aligned with the General Staff, being directly responsible for military operations, had little contact with the Japanese public; they were primarily concerned with achieving military superiority and, ultimately, victories in the field. Those officers who were assigned to the War Ministry, however, dealt with the Japanese government; having to negotiate with politicians and obtain approval of the Diet (the Japanese legislative body), they had to deal with the desires of the general populace. From the nature of their work, then, officers in the War Ministry tended to be more sympathetic and subservient to the will of the public. Invari-

I

Credits for pictures on the following seven pages, covering the background and trial of General Tomoyuki Yamashita:

Page II

Top and bottom: Japanese atrocities in Manila, February 23, 1945 *(US Army Photograph)*

Page III

Top: Japanese atrocities in Manila; picture of Angel Gajo, 38, who was bound and left to burn with his house when he refused to leave it; miraculously and despite severe burns, he was able to crawl out of the flaming house *(US Army Photograph)*

Bottom: rape and bayonet victim of Manila *(US Army Photograph)*

Page IV

Top left: General Yamashita leads his staff down the trail to surrender to U.S. forces in Kiangan, northern Luzon *(US Army Photograph)*

Top right: The gates of Manila's New Bilibid Prison close behind Yamashita, where he arrives from Baguio a few hours after signing surrender documents *(US Army Photograph; Photograph: Potter)*

Bottom: Yamashita, utilizing a G.I. helmet, washes his hands after his surrender; he was scheduled to sign surrender documents the following day *(US Army Photograph; Photographer: Christopher)*

Page V

Top: members of the U.S. military commission for the Yamashita trial from left to right: Brig. Gen. Morris C. Handwerk, Maj. Gen. Donovan, Maj. Gen. Royal Reynolds, Maj. Gen. James A. Lester, and Brig. Gen. Lathrop R. Bullene *(US Army Photograph: Photographer: Mayers)*

Bottom: Yamashita defense counsel from left to right: Col. H. F. Clarke, Capt. A. Frank Reel, Lt. Col. W. C. Hendrix, and Capt. Milton Sandberg *(US Army Photograph)*

Page VI

Top: Yamashita and interpreter speak; Capt. Reel is seen in the background *(US Army Photograph)*

Bottom: General Yamashita is arraigned before the war crimes tribunal; commission members from left to right are: Brig. Gen. Bullene, Maj. Gen. C. L. Sturdevant, Maj. Gen. R. B. Reynolds, Maj. Gen. J. A. Lester, and Brig. Gen. W. G. Walker *(US Army Photograph)*

Page VII

Top left: Yamashita and counsel *(US Army Photograph)*

Top right: Yamashita speaks in his own behalf *(US Army Photograph; Photographer: Farrand)*

Bottom: Yamashita hears the sentence of the court *(National Archives)*

Page VIII

Yamashita took his last thirteen steps to the top of this gallows *(UPI Photo)*

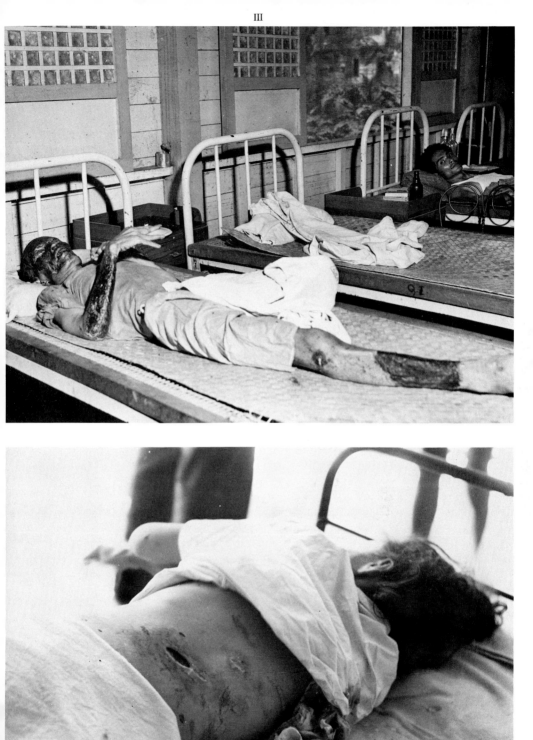

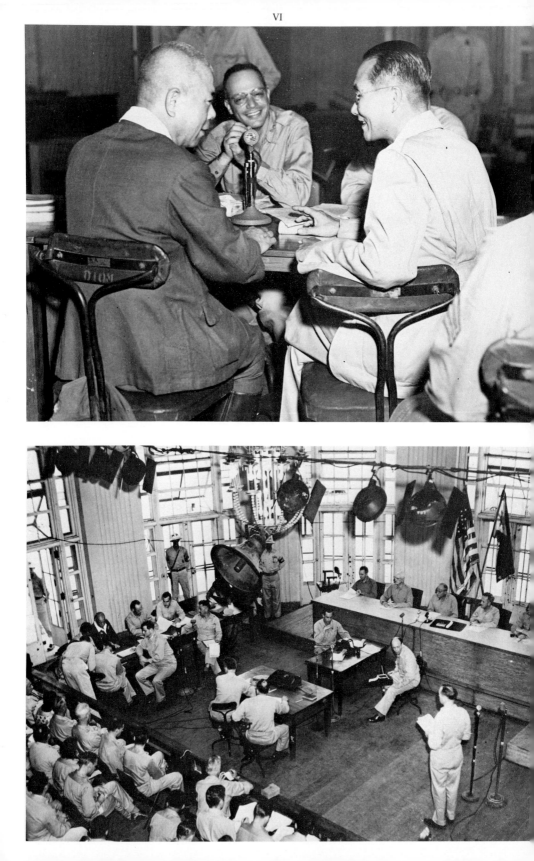

ably, the General Staff found itself opposed to the policies of the War Ministry.

In 1929, General Kazushige Ugaki was the Japanese war minister. Public opinion was strongly opposed to war and against any military buildup or activity that would threaten war. Yet the increasingly powerful factions within the army—particularly the Control Faction of Colonel Tojo—were adamantly committed to expanding the army and invading China and Korea. And it was into this breach that Yamashita was now thrust.

As a member of the ministry's War Affairs Section, dealing with mobilization and budget, Yamashita drafted a radical plan of disarmament. He bluntly proposed an unheard-of reduction of men and weapons within the army, lowering it to a strength "adequate for defensive purposes only." He submitted the draft to Ugaki, who approved it; within weeks, the "Ugaki Plan" was adopted by the Diet, much to the anger of the General Staff.

Tojo was not to forget. When Ugaki was later appointed premier of Japan, the army refused to name a war minister to the cabinet. Thus, unable to serve without a cabinet and unable to return effectively to military command, Ugaki was forced into retirement. He was later to remember Yamashita as "a strong character, clean and honest and of a kindly and gentle disposition . . . well thought of by the people, and the type of man needed for the future of the country."

Tojo, by now a lieutenant general and in effective control of the Japanese military, turned his attentions to the man who had tried to decimate Japan's military ambitions. In 1936, Yamashita, now a major general, was transferred out of the War Ministry and assigned to command an infantry brigade in Korea. Though considered a brilliant strategist and leader, he was then further isolated by being sent to remote stations in North China and

Manchuria. He remained in these lonely outposts until 1940.

Yamashita was to suffer from the powerful Tojo's antipathy for the rest of his career. But he refused to complain. "I have nothing against General Tojo," he would say simply. "Apparently he has something against me."

Again anxious to have Yamashita's influence far removed from Tokyo, Tojo ordered the general to tour Europe for six months as part of a small military group to inspect German and Italian armament. It was while homeward bound from this trip that Yamashita heard of Germany's invasion of Russia. All of the officers in the military mission predicted a quick German victory—all but one. Yamashita argued that the Wehrmacht would be successful at first but that the front was too large, that the campaign would become prolonged, and that Russia could hold out longer and would prove victorious in the end.

The German invasion prompted Yamashita to make another dire prediction: If war with America were to occur, Japan would lose. As his aide later wrote, Yamashita felt that "judging from the national strength and condition of armament of the Japanese nation, it was imperative that Japan should bring the China incident to an immediate close and place the relations with America and Great Britain on a peaceful basis."

When word of Yamashita's latest antiaggression stance reached the General Staff, he was again sent off into isolation. In September of 1941, he was transferred to Manchukuo to assume the relatively unimportant command of the Kwantung Army. There, it was felt, his subversive views of peace would not undermine the morale of fellow officers. For the military machine, now fully in control of the government, was deeply committed to an expansion of the Japanese empire into a "Greater East Asia Co-Prosperity Sphere."

Yamashita did not sit in Manchukuo for long. War with America and Great Britain was now inevitable, and leaders of Yamashita's abilities could not be wasted. Two months after his banishment, he was recalled by the General Staff and summoned to the offices of General Sugiyama. There, with General Homma and General Imamura, he learned of his assignment to the command of the 25th Army. His mission—to capture as much of Malaya as possible and then hold until reinforcements arrived.

Yamashita was not expected to capture the British stronghold at Singapore. The British fortress there, like the American one on Corregidor, was generally considered impregnable. General Percival commanded an army of over 100,000 men, many of them firmly entrenched on the island-city with huge cannons. Yamashita would have only 30,000 men, and so he was told by Sugiyama to fight his way down the Malayan peninsula, holding as much of the mineral-rich land as possible while diverting Allied strength from other theatres of operation.

But the British made the first of two fatal errors; they positioned all of their big guns facing out to sea, expecting the invasion to come by amphibious assault. The jungles of Malaya, it was felt, would prove impenetrable by a large army. "The bloody Japs must attack from the water," one English officer reasoned. "They wouldn't come down from the north because, well, because we wouldn't do it that way."

Yamashita's forces landed along the unguarded beaches, then quickly worked their way down the coastlines in small boats during the nighttime. The British outposts were largely bypassed. And within weeks Yamashita's entire force of 30,000 men was massed outside of the city, threatening Singapore from the land side and rendering the fixed guns useless.

The British now made their second critical mistake, a mistake ironically similar to that made by MacArthur in

Manila. Flooded with reports from around the peninsula of large Japanese troop movements and confronted now with a concentrated force at Singapore's gates, General Percival assumed he was facing a superior force. Certainly, it made sense. The Japanese would not send an inferior force against 100,000 men in a fortified garrison. Percival had to make a decision: Could his 100,000 men hold out, without reinforcements or further supplies, or would he be risking annihilation of the army as well as of the city's civilian population?

Percival asked for a surrender conference. Within hours, Percival and Yamashita were face-to-face in a cashier's cage of a Singapore bank. Dozens of reporters and photographers stood anxiously outside of the wire enclosure, trying to see what was going on between the two men and their interpreters.

Yamashita later recalled feeling truly frightened. He knew he was outnumbered by more than three-to-one; he could only hope that a surrender could be negotiated before the British discovered the true size of Yamashita's army. "I felt that if we had to fight in the city," Yamashita recalled, "we would be beaten. I offered surrender terms to spare the city, but, first of all, the surrender had to be *at once*. I insisted that the cease-fire order be effective at six o'clock that very evening."

Yamashita realized that if the surrender were not effected immediately, the British were likely to discover his numerical weakness during scouting forays that night. Then he would be in danger of being wiped out by a massive British counteroffensive.

Yamashita appeared calm, his stoic face hiding the anxiety inside, as his interpreter continued to explain the terms of surrender to the British commander. Percival appeared to be stalling, as the conversation between him and the interpreter dragged on.

Finally, Yamashita shook his finger at his interpreter.

"There is no need for all this talk. It is a simple question, and I want a simple answer: yes or no."

The newsmen watched the scene, watched the powerfully built general shaking his finger. They could not understand Japanese, but they made out the "yes or no."

Suddenly, Percival nodded. The answer was yes. Singapore was surrendered. And the newsmen had a second story—the "Tiger of Malaya." Unfortunately, as is so often true, it was not accurately descriptive but rather simply catch-phrase journalism. Yamashita was no tiger but a gentle, reflective man. Like Homma, he was a brilliant leader and tactician yet a quiet, introspective person. But at the trial four years later, he would still be referred to as the "Tiger of Malaya."

Yamashita became an instant national hero in Japan. He had conquered the "impregnable" Singapore with a vastly smaller force. He was widely hailed as a genius, and his swift campaign in Malaya as one of the most brilliant in military history. A joyful government announced that every family would receive two bottles of beer and a packet of beans to celebrate; each child was to receive a box of cakes and candy. But Yamashita drew back from the accolades. The conquest of Singapore had *not* been brilliant, he insisted: "It was a bluff," he said, "a bluff that worked."

Meanwhile, the Allied governments managed to suppress the facts. Singapore had fallen, the newspapers read, but the valiant garrison had been overwhelmed by hordes of Japanese soldiers. It was not until after the war was over that *Life* magazine published the text of a secret speech delivered by Prime Minister Winston Churchill to the House of Commons soon after the defeat. "Singapore, with a force of 100,000 men," he admitted reluctantly, "surrendered to 30,000 Japanese." He advised against an investigation of the "debacle," saying it would "hamper the prosecution of the war."

And so, as with Bataan, the facts of an embarrassing defeat were hushed up, and tales of Allied heroism against unending waves of crazed, sadistic Japanese soldiers took their place in the newspapers and on the motion-picture screen. But the simple and undeniable truth was that the British prisoners were treated humanely, and no "war crimes" were even alleged against Yamashita for his brilliant victories in Malaya.

Yamashita was a hero, his name on the lips of every Japanese citizen. But he was to be an absentee hero. Jealous of his enemy's new fame, Tojo denied him even the traditional honor of personally making his report to the emperor. Instead, Tojo again shunted Yamashita off into the remote hinterlands. Again, he was transferred to an unimportant post deep in Manchukuo, with specific orders not to stop over in Japan on his way to his new command.

Thus, in a continuing parallel with the tragic story of Masaharu Homma, Yamashita spent most of the war drilling his troops meaninglessly in a barren land thousands of miles from any combat. Two of the most brilliant leaders in the Japanese Army had run afoul of the all-powerful Hideki Tojo.

Two-and-a-half years passed, and Yamashita listened in Manchukuo to the steady stream of bad news. As he had predicted, Japan was losing the war. Then, with the fall of Saipan in July of 1944, Tojo and his cabinet resigned from office. Peleliu fell in September, and it became clear that the Philippines would be next.

With Tojo gone from power, Yamashita was again recalled from his lonely outpost. His assignment: to take command of the 14th Army in the Philippines. After only four days of briefing in Tokyo, he was rushed to Manila to relieve Lieutenant General Kuruda.

Yamashita found the Japanese defenses to be in bad shape. Forces were scattered, supplies were low, and the command structure was seriously broken into fragments. Most importantly, reinforcements were desperately needed.

He began reorganizing the defenses immediately. With the help of his new chief of staff, Lieutenant General Muto, he hurriedly began shoring up defenses and reviewing the battle plans. But it was already too late. MacArthur landed on Leyte on December 7.

The scene was now set for the tragedy that was soon to unfold in Manila.

It is perhaps interesting to note, as the atrocities were to begin, General Muto's later analysis of his new commander. While undoubtedly couched in exaggeration, it tends at the least to illustrate the devotion Yamashita inspired in his men.

> The personality and character of General Yamashita are the combined products of his natural traits, his education and training, and his subsequent career as a soldier. In analyzing the character of General Yamashita, one must not overlook the influence of harmony and order which are the fundamental laws of nature herself and which are so manifest in the hills and streams of his childhood days and youth. Strife and greed and ugliness are qualities which the General detests most in man, and there are few among his compatriots who are so natural, so unassuming, so little given to worldly ambition. . . . An inherent trust in fellow beings is a quality found only in souls which are themselves pure and good, and by anyone who has been fortunate enough to come into contact with the big heart and upright character of this man this truth is quickly found out.

6
The Rape of a City

MacArthur set about recapturing his beloved Philippine Islands with a vengeance. In a sense, the entire war for him had been geared to this moment. He had been beaten, for the first time in his life, on Bataan, and he had been forced to run away in disgrace from the battle, abandoning his men to their eventual fate on the Death March. Just as bad, he had deserted the Filipino people, who had grown to trust him and look to him as some kind of national savior. The Philippines was more than a command post to MacArthur; it was an adopted homeland. In any event, there was more in MacArthur's mind as he stepped onto the sandy beaches of Leyte than just another military campaign. Undoubtedly, there was the memory of defeat, of desertion, of charges of cowardice; there was revenge; there was vindication.

The amphibious assault on Leyte went forward on a massive scale. Against minimal resistance, MacArthur's

114

huge armada landed hundreds of assault boats, carrying division after division of American soldiers onto Philippine soil. MacArthur himself later wrote that he had gone in with the "third assault wave." In reality, he waited aboard ship until the beachhead was secured and the invasion was three hours old. Photographers were carefully arranged to record the historic event as the colorful general made good his promise to return. Later, he repeated the dramatic landing for additional photographers, the look on his face even more grim and determined than before.

MacArthur recalled, "It took me only 30 or 40 long strides to reach dry land, but that was one of the most meaningful walks I ever took. When it was done, and I stood on the sand, I knew I was back again—against my old enemies of Bataan, for there, shining on the bodies of dead Japanese soldiers, I saw the insignia of the 16th Division, General Homma's ace unit."

MacArthur kicked several of the fresh corpses over with his toe. "The 16th Division," he muttered to a reporter. "They're the ones that did the dirty work on Bataan." In fact, the 16th Division had not been involved in the Death March, but the statement was indicative of MacArthur's frame of mind.

Meanwhile, the invasion continued on a massive scale. Hundreds of thousands of soldiers landed on Leyte, backed by endless armadas of warships and airplanes. With the exception of foredoomed Japanese naval attacks and *kamikaze* crashes, the sea and air belonged to MacArthur. And on the Philippines, his vast superiority in manpower and weapons soon took their toll. Slowly, the badly outnumbered and undersupplied Japanese forces fell back in the face of the overwhelming onslaught of men, planes, and tanks.

The American soldiers had no mercy on their beaten Japanese counterparts. The cry of *Bataan* and *Corregidor* was fresh in their ears, and army propaganda posters urged them to give no quarters to the "yellow bastards." Grisly field executions, even torture, were not unheard of as MacArthur's forces overran the weak Japanese defenses. Charles Lindbergh was later to observe in his *Wartime Diaries:* "Our men think nothing of shooting a Japanese prisoner or soldier attempting to surrender. They treat the Jap with less respect than they would give an animal, and these acts are condoned by almost everyone. We claim to be fighting for civilization, but the more I see of this war in the Pacific the less right I think we have to claim to be civilized. In fact, I am not sure our record in this respect stands so much higher than the Japs."

Steadily, the outnumbered and disorganized Japanese forces retreated or were annihilated before the clearly superior American forces. MacArthur was to characterize this as a brilliant victory. He was later to write of the one-sided contest: "They were unable to conduct an orderly retreat, in classic fashion, to fall back on inner perimeters with forces intact for a last defense. . . . It was a situation unique in modern war. Never had such a large number of troops been so outmaneuvered . . . and left tactically impotent to take an active part in the final battle for their homeland."

And so MacArthur steadily wore on toward his goal to the north—Manila.

Yamashita was, of course, in an impossible situation. He commanded about 100,000 men in the northern Luzon area, less than a fourth of the number now converging on him under MacArthur's command. Worse than this, however, was the simple fact that he had no protection from air bombardment and no supply lines by sea. He soon found that he could not even step outside of his headquarters except at night because of the constant bombardments and strafings. His men were short of food and ammunition, but the few supply ships sent from Japan were almost always sunk trying to run the gauntlet of American submarines, airplanes, and warships.

Perhaps most importantly, Yamashita had simply not had time to familiarize himself with Philippine geography and with the quality and condition of his army. When he was informed that MacArthur's troops had landed on Leyte, he had replied, "Very interesting, but where is Leyte?"

He had had no time to review the structure and condition of his command. The enemy had landed, and they were advancing everywhere in overwhelming strength. His orders were clear, if not realistic—eliminate the enemy. He was instructed from Tokyo to send immediately "the greatest possible troop strength" to reinforce the retreating units on Leyte. Yamashita objected, quickly realizing that MacArthur's massive forces would crush anything he could muster; a deep knowledge of geography was not needed to understand that the mountains to the north of Manila offered better chances of defense than the open plains of Leyte and Luzon to the south.

But the orders stuck, and Yamashita tried to carry them out. He gathered together units that had been dispersed almost haphazardly around Luzon; he fought with the naval command to get transport ships; and he even succeeded in commandeering a few remaining planes from the air force to give the ships air cover. Finally, he was able to put fifty thousand men on ships bound for Leyte. Within days, over half of those men were drowned in the Sibuyan sea, victims of American airplanes and submarines.

Yamashita later recalled his difficulties:

> I was naturally unprepared for the sudden change in our overall defense plans and experienced tremen-

dous difficulty in the successful execution of this
new order. The problem of assembling the widely
dispersed units originally intended for the defense
of Luzon, the drawing-up and execution of new disposition of troops, the reconcentration and rear-
rangement of war-material depots, the mobilization
of transport facilities, the consultation and arrange-
ment with the navy and the air force command for
convoy and aerial protection, and other complex
problems connected with having to organize and
transfer a large army composed of units under diver-
sified command to a new battlefield were multifari-
ous and difficult to solve, and, in spite of my anxiety
for quick action, progress was slow and far from
meeting requirements. The transports which were
massed through admirable efforts on the part of my
subordinates were, with a few exceptions, practically
all sunk or damaged by the American air force en
route, and it was my misfortune to receive discour-
aging reports of these disasters day after day. However, my orders were such that I was obliged to
draw up new shipping plans to meet the critical situation in Leyte. I was so occupied with these difficult problems that I had hardly time to turn my attention to other business.

Yamashita realized that trying to defend Leyte was suicidal. He radioed Field Marshall Terauchi, pleading with
the Japanese supreme commander to let him abandon the
indefensible Leyte as a lost cause and concentrate on defending Luzon against the inevitable second invasion. Terauchi curtly replied, "Muster all strength to totally destroy the enemy of Leyte." Yamashita could not believe
it. Was it possible the high command seriously believed
his weakened, disorganized, outnumbered troops could
really defeat the American onslaught? "I fully understand
your intention," Yamashita wired back, "and will carry it
out to a successful end." Soon after sending this message, he received word that Admiral Halsey's carrier

planes had attacked a convoy off Leyte, and 10,000 more soldiers had drowned.

Finally, Imperial Headquarters realized that Leyte was lost. They reluctantly permitted Yamashita to concentrate his available defenses on Luzon. But irrevocable damage had been done. Already a fraction of the size of MacArthur's force, Yamashita's army had been further depleted in the costly and futile attempt to defend Leyte. Quite simply, the General Staff had not been able to accept the loss of any Philippine soil to the Americans, and their blindness to reality had cost Yamashita dearly.

As mid-December of 1944 arrived, Yamashita turned his attentions to the defense of Luzon. His forces were so weakened that he knew Luzon was almost defenseless from invasion. He begged Terauchi for reinforcements. Three fresh divisions of boys and old men were shipped from Japan. Almost two-thirds of them were sent to the bottom of the Philippine Sea.

Yamashita realized that MacArthur was free to choose any landing point on Luzon he wished. Without naval or air forces, and with inferior army units, an invasion could not be opposed. The landing operation could be successfully completed "with absolute certainty." And once the landing had been achieved, MacArthur's superior strength, mobility, firepower, and air cover would prevent Yamashita from resisting him on flat land. As Yamashita later described his simple strategy: "In view of the Leyte operations I realized that a decisive battle was impossible. Therefore, I decided on a delaying action to divert American forces in Luzon so as to keep them from attacking Japan as long as possible. In my experience with the Leyte operations I realized that the American air forces and navy were exceedingly superior to ours and also the firepower of the ground forces was superior and very mobile. Therefore, I knew that I could not conduct warfare on flat land. So I decided to employ a delaying action in the mountains."

MacArthur's forces soon landed on Luzon and immediately began pressing toward Manila. Yamashita gathered his remaining army and pulled out of the city, heading for the northern mountains. "I decided to put Manila outside the battle area," Yamashita later recalled. "I ordered my troops out of Manila. I decided to abandon it without a battle. There were three reasons for this decision. First, the population of Manila is approximately one million; therefore, it is impossible to feed them. The second reason is that the buildings are very inflammable. The third reason is that because it is flat land it requires tremendous strength to defend it."

And so, as MacArthur had calmly predicted to the news reporters that accompanied him everywhere, Yamashita withdrew his troops from the city, declaring that "the capital of the republic and its law-abiding inhabitants should not suffer from the ravages of war."

MacArthur's aides prepared for the victorious entry into Manila, complete with plans for "a great victory parade à la Champs-Élysées." MacArthur was arranging the entry for January 26th, his sixty-fifth birthday. Although this proved overly optimistic, by February 3, advance cavalry units had entered the city limits, and MacArthur was able to announce confidently, "Our forces are rapidly clearing the enemy from Manila. Our converging columns . . . entered the city and surrounded the Jap defenders. Their complete destruction is imminent." Within a few days, the American media was informed Manila had been taken; *Newsweek*'s February 12th headline read "Prize of the Pacific War, Manila Fell to MacArthur Like Ripened Plum."

But it had not fallen. It was not to fall for over a month. And during that bloody one-month period, Manila was to be the scene of mass murders and atrocities committed against the Filipino people on an almost unheard-of scale.

As the American army had advanced on Manila, it had begun overrunning Japanese prisoner-of-war camps. And emerging from behind the barbed-wire fences were thin, gaunt bodies and hollow-cheeked, vacant-eyed faces. Quickly, the stories began to spread—the American and Filipino POWs had been starved, hundreds had died of malnutrition, hundreds others from untreated wounds and disease. Unfortunately, the stories were true.

MacArthur personally visited the prison camps. First at Bilibid, then at Santo Tomás, he watched as the thin, hungry men dressed in rags were freed from their enclosures. He later wrote: "I looked down the lines of men bearded and soiled . . . with ripped and soiled shirts and trousers, with toes sticking out of such shoes as remained, with suffering and torture written on their gaunt faces. Here was all that was left of my men of Bataan and Corregidor."

Unlike what was about to happen in Manila, Yamashita was vaguely aware of the conditions in the prisoner-of-war camps. Over 10,000 men were interned in the camps, and most of these men received a diet consisting primarily of rice—and a small one at that. Rarely did they receive medicine for their illnesses and wounds. But there was little Yamashita could do about it.

The simple fact was that the POWs received approximately the same ration of available food as did the Japanese soldier. Under the Geneva Convention, prisoners are to be issued the same rations as the captor's own soldiers, and this was exactly what was done. Unfortunately, MacArthur's air and sea forces were so effective that supplies to Yamashita were all but cut off. For example, only one single shipment of rice arrived safely during the one-year period from the invasion of Leyte to final surrender; this one shipment was all that was available to feed 10,000 prisoners and 100,000 Japanese soldiers for a year! Instead, Yamashita's army found itself having to forage through the countryside for anything that was edible. Most Japanese soldiers were suffering from some stage of malnutrition, many of them actually in advanced stages of starvation. Yamashita himself lost a considerable amount of weight during this period, refusing to eat full rations when his men did not have them. Similarly, medicine and new clothing were almost nonexistent; Japanese soldiers were dying of untreated wounds and diseases right along with American and Filipino prisoners, and their uniforms often consisted of nothing but rags.

As General Muto later reflected sardonically, "Although in the latter part of December, Manila Bay had been rendered impossible of access and egress of Japanese vessels, Marshal Terauchi had arranged to send to San Fernando approximately ten thousand tons of rice and ten or more thousands of drums of gasoline, and we were awaiting these supplies with much joy. However, instead of the rice coming ashore, the American Army came ashore."

Clearly, the prisoners in the camps were underfed. Just as clearly, the Japanese soldiers in the field were also underfed. And there was nothing Yamashita could do about it. Yet the charge of starving prisoners was later to be added to the list of his war crimes.

Yamashita transferred his headquarters from Fort McKinley, near Manila, to Baguio, a city high in the mountains north of Manila. In obedience to his express orders, his army units withdrew from Manila, leaving the city physically intact and its inhabitants unharmed. Roughly 100,000 men straggled slowly in retreat toward the protective mountains of northern Luzon, leaving behind them the capital of the Philippines. Only 1,600 of Yamashita's men remained behind in the city, with specific orders to guard those military supplies that had not yet been moved; with gasoline and transport trucks in short supply, Yamashita was experiencing difficulty in moving equipment, weapons, and ammunition out of the city. When the supplies could be transported, the small contingent of soldiers was to accompany them to the mountains; if they could not be rescued before MacArthur's arrival, the supplies were to be destroyed.

But Yamashita's handful of soldiers was not alone in Manila. With them in the city were 20,000 Japanese naval personnel—sailors and marines from a small group of warships in Manila Harbor commanded by Admiral Sanji Iwabuchi. Technically, this naval force was under the command of Yamashita; they were considered to be engaged while ashore in land operations and therefore under the limited command of the army. Accordingly, Yamashita sent an order to Admiral Iwabuchi, directing him to evacuate his men from the city at the same time as the army withdrew.

Iwabuchi now faced a critical decision. Unknown to Yamashita, he had been ordered by Vice-Admiral Desuchi Okuchi to destroy all naval facilities in Manila, rendering the harbor unfit for use by the Americans. In even stronger language, Vice-Admiral Gunichi Mikawa had instructed him that he was to fight MacArthur "to the death." Yet Yamashita was technically his immediate commander and had ordered him to abandon Manila, leaving it untouched and without a fight.

It is not known how long or how seriously Iwabuchi pondered this decision or what factor the traditional hatred between the army and navy played in his decision. What is known is that Iwabuchi issued orders to his 20,000 men ashore to defend the city. He commandeered Yamashita's 1,600 soldiers, and makeshift fortifications were built to face MacArthur's onslaught.

It was not until February 13th that Yamashita learned

from General Yokoyama, commanding a rear-guard holding force to cover the retreat, that naval men were still in
Manila. Infuriated, Yamashita ordered his general to get
the sailors out of the city "in accordance with our original
plan." But by now it was too late. MacArthur's forces
had completely surrounded Manila, cutting the naval
units and the small contingent of soldiers off from Yamashita's control. The troops in Manila were trapped.

Yokoyama attempted a daring attack on the American
perimeter in an attempt to break through, but succeeded
only in sustaining heavy casualties. Iwabuchi's force was
now cut off from any communications with Yamashita;
there was no way that Yamashita could rescue any of the
men or even know what was happening within the city.

Some of MacArthur's huge force branched off from the
advance on Manila and pursued Yamashita's retreating
forces. While Yokoyama's small unit was able to slow
many of them down, others managed to make contact
with the main force and engage the Japanese in combat
during the desperate retreat into the mountains. Long-
range artillery pounded Yamashita's troops, and hundreds of warplanes bombed and strafed the defenseless
soldiers with immunity. Added to this, Filipino guerrilla
bands were actively sabotaging supplies and roads and
destroying all means of telephone communication. As
General Marshall was later to report, Yamashita's command was disrupted into isolated units, and he "was
forced into a piecemeal commitment of his troops."

Meanwhile, the surrounded Iwabuchi issued further
orders to the sailors, marines, and small band of
soldiers—lay waste to the city! The men were instructed
that they were to die for the emperor but that their
deaths should be paid for in enemy lives. Beer, *sake,* and
wine from Manila's shops were distributed to the men,
and within hours the 20,000-man force was a raging,
drunken mob.

In an intoxicated fury of revenge and despair, the wild-eyed sailors threw themselves into an orgy of burning, shooting, raping, and torture. Young girls and old women were raped and then beheaded; men's bodies were hung in the air and mutilated; babies' eyeballs were ripped out and smeared across walls; patients were tied down to their beds and then the hospital burned to the ground. The atrocities continued on seemingly without end, as the American troops fought to breach the naval forces' perimeters. Iwabuchi did nothing to stop the nightmare and, in fact, apparently actively encouraged it.

MacArthur's soldiers struggled to root out the fanatic Japanese sailors, fighting them in hand-to-hand combat from building to building throughout the city. Finally, the Japanese survivors retreated into the old walled city of Intramuros, protected by huge stone walls forty feet thick. They were eventually blasted out after repeated heavy artillery barrages.

With Manila almost under control, MacArthur drove into the center of the city. He was anxious to return to the penthouse atop the Manila Hotel, which had for so long been his home and office. As he approached the hotel, a busboy told him that the penthouse was undamaged but still in Japanese hands. "Suddenly," MacArthur recalled, "the penthouse blazed into flame. They had fired it. I watched, with indescribable feelings, the destruction of my fine military library, my souvenirs, my personal belongings of a lifetime. . . . I was tasting to the last acid dregs the bitterness of a devastated and beloved home."

One of MacArthur's aides described the scene as MacArthur entered the burned-out penthouse, stepping over the bodies of Japanese sailors. "The books were still on the bookshelves. You could read the titles on the spines, but when you touched them, they just disintegrated. I thought of that later, during the trouble with the Huks and in the old European colonies—Vietnam, Malaysia, Burma and the rest. It was as though pre-war Asia was coming apart before our eyes. I think the General felt a little that way, too, at the time. Maybe that's one reason why he was so upset during the [liberation] ceremony later at Malacanan [Palace]."

By the time the American forces were able to kill the last Japanese sailor—Iwabuchi included—nearly 60,000 Filipinos lay dead. Three-fourths of the factories and homes had been leveled, and the entire business district of Manila had been destroyed. Manila had almost ceased to exist as a city. Its destruction and the unimaginable atrocities committed against thousands of its inhabitants would long be remembered as one of the most tragic and heinous incidents in the annals of "civilized" warfare.

The question of responsibility remained.

Book Three: Justice

7
War Crimes

ON SEPTEMBER 2, 1945, GENERAL MACARTHUR ACCEPTED the Japanese surrender aboard the U. S. battleship *Missouri* in Tokyo Bay. After the ceremonies were concluded, he informed the gathered press: "As Supreme Commander for the Allied Powers, I announce it my firm purpose, in the tradition of the countries I represent, to proceed in the discharge of my responsibilities with justice and tolerance." Standing ominously at his side as these words were being read were the two Allied commanders who, along with MacArthur, had suffered the most humiliating defeats of the war—General Wainwright and the British General Percival.

MacArthur wasted no time in meting out justice, if not tolerance. A directive of the U. S. Joint Chiefs of Staff had, at MacArthur's request, ordered the investigation and detention of all Japanese suspected of war crimes. It specifically empowered MacArthur to set up special international courts for the trial of those charged and to prescribe the rules of procedure to be followed by them.

Armed with this authority, MacArthur quickly established two separate war-crimes offices. The first was called the "International Prosecution Section" and was intended to bring to justice the major Japanese war criminals, starting with Hideki Tojo. To facilitate this prosecution, MacArthur created the International Military Tribunal for the Far East to sit in judgment in Tokyo. Essentially, it was similar to the Nazi trials at Nuremburg and consisted of a panel of independent judges from eleven Allied nations.

The second office set up by MacArthur was the War Crimes Branch of the U. S. General Headquarters of the Army Forces in the Pacific, with branches based in Yokohama and in Manila. The purpose of this military prosecuting agency was to investigate and bring to trial all war criminals not considered "major" enough for the inclusion in the Tokyo trials. The judicial body for these trials was to consist of U. S. Army officers appointed by MacArthur.

The differences between the procedures followed by the two separate war-crimes systems were considerable. The major war criminals—Tojo and twenty-seven other political and military leaders—were afforded every conceivable procedural safeguard. The panel of judges was composed of brilliant legal minds, many of them from the supreme courts of their respective nations. Evidentiary rules and legal procedures were strictly observed, and no pressure was, or could be, brought to bear on the justices. Aside from establishing the proceeding, MacArthur took little part. The charges were specified in detail, and ample time was given the defense for preparation of its case. In fact, the trials did not begin until May 3, 1946 and continued on for two-and-a-half years.

The trials that were to take place in MacArthur's adopted home of Manila, however, were to prove another matter altogether. There, the stage was being very quickly set for the trials of the two men responsible for Bataan and Manila. Yamashita was charged with war crimes three *weeks* after the surrender, and the trial was set to begin three weeks after that.

General MacArthur, as supreme commander, was, of course, the fountainhead of all authority in the Far East. He was responsible for administering the government of Japan, as well as the continued command of the Allied military forces. Despite awesome and time-consuming tasks, his attentions were immediately directed to the prosecution of two Japanese generals.

MacArthur turned first to the matter of General Tomo- yuki Yamashita, for Manila was still fresh in his mind. He quickly appointed six military lawyers from the Judge Ad- vocate's Department to serve as the prosecution team; in fact, this was done even before the Japanese surrender. Chief of the prosecution staff was Major Robert Kerr, an infantry officer who had been a lawyer in Portland. Tall and debonair, with a small, black mustache, Kerr liked to distinguish himself from his fellow prosecutors. They were lawyers, he would say, but he was a combat soldier. Although he had never actually seen any combat, Kerr was later to tell a reporter that he had come to the Far East expecting "to shoot Japs on the beaches rather than hang them, but it was all the same" to him. Fortunately for Kerr, his staff of prosecutors—Captains Hill, Webster, Pace, and Calyer—had all been district attorneys before entering the army and were to prove able and experienced criminal attorneys. The sixth member, Major Glicerio Opinión, was a political appointment; MacArthur felt it wise to give the Filipino people some representation in the prosecution. Opinión was, however, to prove a bumbling fool in trial. When told by one witness that her baby had been a male, Opinión repeated, "I see, a male. And was it a son or a daughter?" Another witness on the stand in- formed Opinión that she was a widow, whereupon the Filipino lawyer replied, "And where is your husband?"

MacArthur realized that a staff of defense lawyers

would have to be appointed to represent Yamashita, but he put this off until the last moment. In fact, the defense lawyers were not named until shortly before the arraignment. It was obvious that Yamashita's newly appointed lawyers would not begin to be able to put together a defense to sixty-two counts of war crimes, any one of which could be punishable by death. As one of the defense attorneys, Captain Reel, later wrote: "We knew that to make even a pretense of investigation of these crimes, involving thousands of people and hundreds of miles of territory, would take many months."

While the appointment of a defense team was held off, MacArthur directed the prosecution staff to begin drafting the charges and gathering the evidence. They were given top priority and all the supplies, manpower, and transportation that was needed. Those in army command realized this was a pet project of MacArthur's and everything should be done to facilitate it. And so, months before the Japanese had surrendered, teams of lawyers and investigators were combing the Philippines, gathering evidence to be used in the trial.

While the prosecuting staff had been hand-picked, however, the defense lawyers were selected almost at random. That they turned out to be talented and totally dedicated men could only have been an accident.

MacArthur had formally delegated responsibility for the conduct of the Homma and Yamashita trials to Lieutenant General Wilhelm D. Styer, the commander of Army Forces, Western Pacific. Styer directed his staff judge advocate, Colonel "Bud" Young, to round up a defense team for Yamashita. Six lawyers were needed. Young looked around his staff and decided he could spare only one man—Lieutenant Colonel James G. Feldhaus, a tax expert from South Dakota. Colonel Feldhaus was soon to become sick and was not to return from the hospital until the end of the trial.

Young then drafted Colonel Harry E. Clarke of Altoona, Pennsylvania, from his job as director of the army's prison in the Philippines. Clarke was to be the senior member of the team, having served in the army since World War I. Unfortunately, as the senior officer he was also the man who was to take the heat from the military judges for the lawyers' attempt to put on a defense for Yamashita.

The next lawyer to be assigned to Yamashita's defense was Lieutenant Colonel Leigh Clark. When he heard of his appointment, Clark became angry and upset. He was a judge in Birmingham, Alabama, and he was afraid he would never be reelected to the bench if his constituency discovered he had defended a Jap war criminal. After a short conference with Colonel Young, Clark was excused from the assignment.

Young next found a lawyer acting as the legal advisor to the military police, Lieutenant Colonel Walter C. Hendrix of Atlanta, Georgia. Hendrix was a big, robust man with strong convictions. When the defense lawyers first met, he loudly proclaimed that he was not happy about the assignment. He would much rather be prosecuting Yamashita. Nevertheless, as the facts became known to the lawyers, Hendrix turned into the most fanatic and reckless defender of them all. He was constantly outraged by the judge's obvious prejudice and was usually in a state of borderline explosion. The judges' consciousness of power was matched only by their ignorance of law, he would say. "No damn general is going to push me around!" was a comment heard muttered frequently from the defense table.

Three more men were needed. Young contacted the Claims Service—where a staff of army lawyers routinely reviewed the thousands of claims of Filipinos for appropriation of, or damage to, their property by the U. S. Army during the war—and informed Colonel Myatt there that three lawyers were to be transferred to his command no later than the following day, and it didn't matter who.

Colonel Myatt was shorthanded as it was, and now he was angry. "They can't have them," he yelled to a subordinate. "How are we going to get our claims settled if they start raiding our personnel?" He instructed Lieutenant Colonel Egner to visit Major General Sturtevant, the army's head of personnel, and explain that the three men could not be spared.

Egner complied, informing Sturtevant that he was sorry but that no lawyers could be spared for the upcoming trial.

"Why not?" Sturtevant asked.

"Well, we haven't enough officers now. We need all we have to do our job as it is."

"Anything else?"

"Yes, Washington just turned down our request for more officers, and we're shorthanded."

"Anything else?" Sturtevant calmly repeated.

"We have a backlog of over 10,000 claims, and General MacArthur wants these claims settled, and we just can't do it if we have to give up any lawyers."

"Anything else?"

"No," Egner replied quietly. "I guess that's all."

"Well, Colonel Egner," Sturtevant said, his voice suddenly rising ominously and his expression turning grim, "I have a piece of paper here. On it are two names. I want a third, and I want it right now!" He pushed a piece of paper across the desk at the startled Egner. On the paper were written the names of Captain Milton Sandberg and Major George Guy, two of the lawyers in the Claims Service.

Shaken, Egner quickly wrote down "Captain A. Frank Reel." Reel had heard of the Yamashita matter and had asked Egner earlier that day not to assign him to it. Flustered by Sturtevant, Egner could think of only one name—Reel.

Again, fate produced three competent lawyers. Major

Guy, from Cheyenne, Wyoming, was a cavalry officer who had served through most of the Pacific campaign. He was an open, colorful individual and proved invaluable in digging up evidence. Captain Milton Sandberg was a young lawyer from New York City. A tax expert like Feldhaus, his trial experience was necessarily limited, but he was to excel in the drafting of legal documents and pleadings. Finally, there was Captain A. Frank Reel, a talented but reluctant lawyer who was soon to find himself devoted to Yamashita's cause.

When Reel heard about the unwanted assignment, he called a friend in MacArthur's Judge Advocate section, Bill Ruddock. Ruddock had already seen the charges that had been prepared against Yamashita and had discussed some of the evidence with the prosecutors. "They have nothing on him at all," Ruddock confided to his friend. "They're trying to establish a new theory—that a commanding officer is responsible if his troops violate the laws of war, regardless of whether he ordered the violations or even knew of them." He paused, then added, "Under such a theory, I guess even MacArthur should be tried."

Having appointed the prosecution, all experienced criminal prosecutors, and delegated the selection of defense counsel, none of whom were criminal lawyers, MacArthur now turned to the composition of the tribunal itself. He would personally select five men to sit on the Military Commission in Manila, five men who would render a verdict as to the guilt of General Yamashita.

Predictably, MacArthur picked five members of the regular army. Three major generals and two brigadier generals would decide the outcome of the case: five professional soldiers whose future careers might well depend on offering no resistance to MacArthur's well-known desires.

The five generals' potential subservience to MacArthur caused Yamashita's counsel enough concern. But another consideration soon came to light: None of the five was a combat man. Each of the generals had been appointed from desk jobs and would be unlikely to understand and appreciate the harsh realities of the conditions with which Yamashita was faced in the battlefield. Major General Russell B. Reynolds, for example, was transferred to the commission from his post as commander of a service unit in Chicago.

Of equal concern to the defense lawyers was the simple fact that none of these men who were to serve as judges were lawyers or had even the slightest legal experience. Yet the general rules established by MacArthur for the conduct of war crimes trials specifically stated, "If feasible, one or more members of a commission should have had legal training." Ominously enough, it had apparently been considered not "feasible" by MacArthur to follow his own rules when it came to Yamashita's trial. For some reason known only to MacArthur, one of the most important of the war crimes trials was going to proceed with a tribunal devoid of any legal knowledge.

General Reynolds was named the president of the commission. Major General Leo Donovan was the next appointee, followed by Major General James A. Lester. Lester had been the head of the military police, and he was to make it clear from the beginning of the trial that he wanted to see Yamashita hang. In fact, newspaper and radio reporters covering the trial jokingly referred to him as "the hanging judge."

The final two judges were Brigadier Generals Bullene and Handwerk. Neither of the two men spoke during the trial, and both were always obediently the last to enter the courtroom and the last to leave, following their three superior officers. The two men seemed to realize their subordinate places, for the trial transcripts are empty of any comments from either of them. Handwerk, particularly, seemed to just gaze out into space during the trial. As one newspaperman wrote, "Someone will have to tell Handwerk when the trial's over, or he'll just keep on coming in every day and won't know the difference."

And so MacArthur had personally selected the five judges, had appointed the prosecutors, and had delegated the selection of the defense lawyers. The judges were career soldiers, likely unwilling to antagonize one of the most powerful men in the U. S. Army. The prosecutors were under MacArthur's military command, as were the defense attorneys. This procedure was soon to be followed in the prosecution against General Homma.

But MacArthur was not finished. He was also personally to draft the criminal procedures to be followed by the commission in conducting the trial, as well as the rules of evidence that would be adhered to. General procedures established by military courtsmartial would not do, nor would civilian criminal procedures. The usual rules of evidence were considered "obstructionist," and the safeguards of the U. S. Constitution were ignored. Article 13 of MacArthur's "Special Proclamation" was clear: "The Tribunal shall not be bound by technical rules of evidence. It shall adopt and apply to the greatest possible extent expeditious and non-technical procedure, and shall admit any evidence which it deems to have probative value. All purported admissions or statements of the accused are admissable." In essence, MacArthur's rules and procedures were simple—anything goes.

There was one technical nicety that he added to the rules, however. And it was a strange one, a rule that had never been seen before. It read: "The official position of the accused shall not absolve him from responsibility, nor be considered in mitigation of punishment. Further, action pursuant to order of the accused's superior, or of his government, shall not constitute a defense." When Captain Reel first read the provision, he could make no sense of it. Then he remembered what his friend had told him about the new theory: Yamashita would be held strictly liable, regardless of circumstances.

Finally, MacArthur established a system of appeals from judgments of conviction. Again, the appellate process was to be very simple. If a defendant was convicted and sentenced to death, there was to be only one source of appeal: General Douglas A. MacArthur.

The stage had been set.

On August 14, 1945, Yamashita's radiomen tuned in on a broadcast from San Francisco announcing that the emperor had surrendered. That evening, Muto assigned a junior officer to sit in Yamashita's room to keep him from committing *seppuku*. But realizing the purpose of his presence, Yamashita calmly explained to the young officer, "Don't worry, I won't go to heaven alone. That'll do no good. My duty is to get the soldiers back home. So relax and go to bed."

A few days later, the commander of the American 32d Division ordered leaflets dropped by plane over Yamashita's position, instructing the Japanese to send an envoy to the American lines to arrange a surrender. On September 1, Yamashita decided to go down personally from his mountain stronghold to surrender. "Any delay is bound to make matters worse for my troops," he explained to Muto. "If I'm wrong about this, then I'll accept the blame. The troops are half-starved, and I want them fed just as soon as possible. I want the sick and wounded attended to also. Every day that the surrender is delayed hundreds more will die."

Yamashita's farewell to his troops was an emotional

scene. Tears were pouring down his face, and his men were crying like children. As the wounded and shabbily dressed headquarters troops were lined up, he went among them and said his good-byes to each man. Finished, he stepped back and saluted. The salute was instantly returned by the men and held as their general slowly walked away from them, heading down the mountain. Three or four times he stopped to glance back at the silent formation of men, then continued on. Finally, after one long, last look at his men, he disappeared from their view.

Yamashita slowly made his way down out of the mountains, supporting a wounded leg with a walking cane. His forces had long since run out of gasoline, and in any event the few vehicles that had escaped Manila had been blown up in the mountains by the swarming American warplanes. Finally, on September 2, he limped calmly into a U. S. Army camp and surrendered his sword to a startled American officer.

Yamashita was not physically the same man as the "Tiger of Malaya." He had lost much weight while starving with his troops in the mountains; his clothes were soiled and ragged, his face was haggard, his eyes tired— tired and sad. He had done his best, but Japan had been defeated. So many of his men had been killed, so much death, starvation, and disease.

Before leaving his headquarters, Yamashita had written a short poem:

> *My men have gathered from the mountains,*
> *Like wild flowers.*
> *Now it is my turn to go,*
> *And I go gladly.*

He had yet to hear of the holocaust that had occurred in Manila.

On September 12, 1945, ten days after the surrender, Masaharu Homma traveled to Sado Island to visit his mother. He spent two days with the old woman and finally left her to return to Tokyo on business. After Tojo's fall from power, Homma had been recalled from his stagnant position in the reserves and appointed information minister in the new government; Homma was to have nothing but an unbroken series of military disasters to report until the end of the war.

As Homma's boat reached the Niigata Pier on the mainland, he and Fujiko were greeted by his third son, a 15-year old schoolboy. Standing by his side was a U. S. Army officer. The officer asked Homma for his identification, then ordered him to accompany him to Tokyo by train; Fujiko was permitted to go with them.

As the train pulled into the station in Tokyo, Homma was surprised to see a crowd of reporters waiting to interview him. After talking with them for a moment, he came back to Fujiko, puzzled.

"They keep asking me about a 'March of Death,'" Homma said to his wife. "What on earth can they mean by that?"

8
U.S.A. v. Yamashita

AFTER YAMASHITA'S SURRENDER, HE WAS QUICKLY whisked away to Government House in Baguio to sign a formal document of surrender. Although the ceremony seemed senseless in view of the general surrender aboard the *Missouri* a few days earlier, there was a point: Across the table from Yamashita, gazing at him over the paperwork, was General Percival. The British general was commanding no units in the Philippines, but MacArthur felt it appropriate and fitting that Percival's earlier humiliating surrender now be cleansed.

After the brief ceremony, Yamashita was taken to New Bilibid Prison in Manila. There he was intensively interrogated by numerous American military personnel. One of them, Lieutenant Commander Samuel Stratton of the U. S. Navy, finally explained the situation to the confused Japanese general—terrible atrocities had been committed against the Filipino people in Manila. Yamashita appeared to be stunned at first, staring in disbelief at the interpreter. Then he was silent, apparently lost in thought.

"If those crimes were committed," he told Stratton, "I positively and categorically affirm that they were against my wishes and in direct contradiction to all my expressed orders." He paused, still trying to grasp what was happening. "If they were committed, they occurred at a place and a time of which I had no knowledge whatsoever." He looked directly at Stratton, then added that had he suspected the atrocities were going to be committed, he would have tried to take steps to prevent them; had he learned of them later, he said, he would have punished those responsible.

The questions went on, day after day, as succeeding shifts of interrogators took their turns in the prison cell with Yamashita. He had still been assigned no lawyer to represent him, nor had any charges yet been drafted. Slowly, he became vaguely aware of the scale of atrocities that had been committed and of how and when they had taken place. But he could not yet understand why he was in prison. Surely, the perpetrators of the atrocities should be punished, but as he understood it, they had all been killed in Manila. Why was *he* being held?

Stratton looked at the interpreter. "Is the general a *samurai*? If so, what were the implications of that status?"

No, Yamashita replied, I am a commoner, the son of a doctor. I might have been a doctor too, he said with a slight smile, had I made better grades in school.

What was the general's religious beliefs? Stratton asked.

"I am a Shintoist," Yamashita said. This cannot be explained easily, he added, nor did he consider himself so pious a man as to think himself able to explain its philosophy in a few words. However, he explained, "there is a divinity which watches over all things and dictates that we humans must be true to a path of righteousness—or to our consciousness of being right—which is the way of heaven."

Stratton nodded, then asked, "When surrender was unavoidable, why didn't the general commit suicide?"

That would have been a violation of the emperor's orders, Yamashita replied through the interpreter. The emperor had commanded his leaders to surrender and to cooperate with the Americans. He had done so.

But, Stratton reminded him, General Tojo had attempted *seppuku* a few days earlier.

Yamashita's expression changed slightly, almost imperceptibly, a distance in his eyes, a hardness to his lips. "Yes," he said, with a trace of scorn, "General Tojo disobeyed the orders of his emperor."

The interrogations continued on for days. Yet, interestingly, no statements ever made at any time by Yamashita were ever introduced into evidence by the prosecution at his trial. Despite thousands of questions posed by dozens of skilled investigators concerning minute details of his command structure, battle orders, knowledge of the circumstances of the retreat from Manila, and conduct of the prisoner-of-war camps, there were simply no inconsistencies, no contradictions, no provable falsehoods. From the very first day of questioning, Yamashita cooperated fully and answered every query. Yet, his detailed answers, which were double-checked against the versions of other witnesses, consistently bore out the simple truth: Yamashita neither ordered nor knew of the atrocities in Manila.

Finally, the Japanese general was handed over to a team of U. S. Army psychiatrists. He was now accompanied by Masakatsu Hamamoto, an aide of Yamashita who was permitted to act as a translator. He had been an officer in the Japanese Army but had graduated from Harvard University in, as he said proudly, "the class of '27." Captain Reel, also a Harvard grad, was to recall "the oriental student who had been in the class ahead of me and whom I had often seen running through the Yard in Cambridge, dressed in tennis shoes." At their first

meeting, Hamamoto was to insist that Reel tell him all
the details of the Harvard tercentenary celebration of
1936, and what had happened to the football teams since
Pearl Harbor.

With Hamamoto interpreting in perfect English, Yamashita replied courteously to the psychiatrists' strange
questions.

Q. Did you eat and sleep well as a child?
A. Yes.
Q. Did you have any fears?
A. No.
Q. Any night terrors or nightmares?
A. No.
Q. Did you bite your fingernails or wet the bed?
A. No.
Q. You were just a happy, carefree youngster with
   no fears at all?
A. Yes.
Q. How do you reconcile your childhood nature of
   being a happy, carefree type of child with the
   decision to go into military life, where you had
   to be harsh and cruel?
A. There is a wide breach in the psychology of the
   Eastern and Western mind on this point. I did not
   feel any inconsistency at heart because of the
   viewpoint or the conception of the role of a soldier in Japan, and that is that they do not consider
   a soldier or a career in the army a more or less
   harsh and cold-blooded profession or calling, although it is true that when fighting each other
   gun to gun they fight very hard. But beyond in-
   flicting death to the other party where both are
   fully armed and on the battlefield, the true soldier
   does not do any harm to any other person, and so
   to the general at that time the military calling was
   not considered a cold-blooded profession and I
   did not feel any inconsistency.

The psychiatrists shifted to the subject of Yamashita's
married life.

Q. When did you get married?

A. 28 years ago. I was 31.

Q. Do you have any reason for not getting married earlier?

A. No particular reason why I married at 31. No particular reason for not marrying earlier. That is the average for marrying in Japan.

Q. How long a courtship did you have?

A. About a year and a half.

Q. Were your parents pleased about your marriage?

A. Both of my parents had died by that time.

Q. Were you happily married?

A. Thank you, very happy.

Q. Do you have a family?

A. Unfortunately, I have no children.

Q. Did that upset or disappoint you?

A. Yes. I had a medical consultation, but nothing could be done.

Q. Is your wife still living?

A. Yes.

Q. Are you and your wife in comfortable circumstances?

A. Ordinary. In other words, not very poor or very rich.

Q. What do you and your wife especially enjoy doing together?

A. Gardening, taking walks together in the mountains, fishing.

Q. Do you like music or dancing?

A. Music, but not dancing. I myself am no musician, but I enjoy listening to music.

And on it went, each psychiatrist probing into the Japanese general, trying to find the psychiatric flaw that would explain how a man could cause the horrible deaths of thousands of helpless civilians.

Q. How does Shintoism make atrocities, murder, rape, etc., possible?

A. Such atrocities are not condoned and should be punished if they do occur.

Q. When they do occur is it because men run wild,
so to speak?

A. I can say very emphatically that a true believer in
Shintoism will not commit such things. Those in
a position to command are responsible for seeing
that such occurrences are prevented and if they
once are aware of it to punish it under military
laws such as we have in our army.

Q. Atrocities are explained on the basis of their perpetrators being under the bad god, Susano.
Could you explain that?

A. Not being a Shinto priest, I am not able to go
into the theology of the matter, but there are
two guiding spirits which control the action of a
human being—the *Nigitarna,* meaning a gentle
spirit, and the *Aratama,* which represents the
rough spirit. I believe this represents the positive and the negative, as we say in scientific
.discussion.

Q. How is it possible to behead a prisoner of war? Is
it compatible with Shintoism?

A. There is no relation whatever with this act of
maltreating a prisoner of war and the teachings
of the Shinto religion. I don't know why they
were beheaded, but there is no direct connection
with Shintoism.

After a few hours, the psychiatrist left, only to be replaced by another army doctor armed with pages of questions. This psychiatrist began immediately probing Yamashita's mind for his attitudes toward the war.

Q. What made you fight the way you did fight?
What is your reaction to war in general?

A. As to war in general, from my study of the history of war I have concluded that in the old days
a war was fought for the whim and fancy of a
local lord, sometimes for more legitimate reasons, but always in the interest of a particular

individual. In modern times I believe that the cause of war is fundamentally economic, an attempt to solve economic needs and allied matters on the part of a nation as a whole—in other words to fulfill the economic requirements of the people as a whole.

Q. What about this war?

A. I believe that the cause of this war is fundamentally economic. In other words, Japan fifty years ago was more or less self-sufficient—the people could live off the land. In that fifty years the population increased to about double so that Japan had to rely on outside sources for food supply and other economic requirements. In her effort to fulfill the new and increased economic requirements which were fundamentally that of feeding the people, she felt it necessary to expand her economic activities outside as well as inside her borders. In order to buy or import her commodities, she had to pay for it ultimately in commodities. This effort on her part was prevented for one reason or another by other countries. Japan made attempts to solve the misunderstandings through peaceful methods, but when all her efforts were either thwarted or negated, in order to sustain the livelihood of her people she felt it necessary to engage in open warfare.

Q. Did all the people in Japan want this war?

A. I have been away from Tokyo for a long time, and I was not there when this war broke out, but to the best of my knowledge I believe that there were many people not in complete accord with having open hostilities. I never believed in this war and thought in my own mind that every effort should have been continued to solve this problem peacefully even to the extent of reducing armament expenses and diverting this fund to industrial development, since the economic well-being of the people was the fundamental question.

Q. If you were not thoroughly sold on this war it is
   amazing that you would be placed in this command. It is not consistent.

A. There would be an inconsistency had I volun-
   teered for any particular command. In my case
   the command came from above; it was my duty
   to assume this position, and as I was trained as a
   soldier I had to be true to my responsibility. I see
   no inconsistency in having fulfilled the particular
   military mission that I was given.

Q. How do you feel about the sneak attack on Pearl
   Harbor and the American idea of fair play?

A. I was not in Tokyo at the time and was not following the developments that led to the war,
   and naturally I am in no position to judge the
   Pearl Harbor attack as a sneak attack or as legitimate tactics, but, generalizing, I would say I
   don't approve of any sneak attacks but that even
   war should be open.

Q. Would you state your opinion regarding the possible prevention of war from now on?

A. I have no master-plan, naturally offhand, of saving the world for peace. I realize the seriousness
   of the problem. All I can say at this time is that
   any plan to insure peace must have as a foundation, first, a practical way in which all the
   peoples of the world can survive on the princi-
   ples of equality, and, second, we must have a
   common conception of what is wrong and adopt
   practical ways and means of disseminating this
   moral concept.

Q. Do you look on the American spirit of fair play
   as a weakness?

A. I believe that the American spirit of fair play is
   the core or the motivating cause for the future
   expansion of America into a greater nation.

Completed with its exhaustive questioning of Yamashita, the team of army psychiatrists drafted its report for
the prosecution. The report began with an acknowledg-
ment that the doctors had been surprised to discover that
Yamashita had responded to their questions with frank-

ness and honesty. "The general appears more as a benign, aging Japanese officer than the formidable 'Tiger of
Malaya,' " the report continued. "He was, throughout
the interview, alert, interested, courteous, and coopera-
tive. One was, against one's will or better judgment, inclined to credit him as being sincere in his answers."

"If we did not have positive knowledge," the report
went on, "of the many instances of documented cruelties
and inhumanities practiced by his soldiers, one would be
inclined to believe his protestations of kindliness and
good sportmanship . . . . In other words, the interview
revealed a lofty, benign code of ethics and behavior quite
the antithesis of actual practice as far as is known." Apparently, the doctors had been convinced by the prosecution before ever meeting Yamashita that he was guilty of
the crimes; the psychiatric questioning had proceeded on
the factual assumption that Yamashita was lying! It is
perhaps a testament to his character that the doctors
could have even reluctantly concluded that he was honest and sincere, acting as they were under the misconcep-
tion that he had committed the atrocities as charged.

General Yamashita was only beginning to experience
the "American spirit of fair play" mentioned by one of
the psychiatrists.

The six defense lawyers met for the first time at New
Bilibid Prison. Perhaps ominously, they were assigned
the prison chapel to use as a conference room. As the
men waited to see what their new client looked like, a
prison officer laughed, "So you're the guys that have to
defend these monkeys, are you?"

Captain Reel recalls waiting in the still chapel. "As we
waited, we wondered what these 'monkeys' would be
like. None of us had ever been well acquainted with any
Japanese. Was the common belief that they were likely to
be tricky, evasive, and unreliable merely propaganda?

Whatever they were, we would be on guard. No polite and clever explanations would fool us. We were as skeptical as only lawyers can be."

As Yamashita walked into the chapel, accompanied by Hamamoto and General Muto, his chief-of-staff, the lawyers were unimpressed. He was a bull-headed man with no neck and narrow, inscrutable eyes; his stoic, unexpressive face surely hid deception behind it. This was the man who was responsible for the terrible atrocities in Manila. Yet as the first interview wore on, the lawyers began to see something else in the aging Japanese general.

"The initial interview," Reel later wrote, "revealed a man of dignity and poise. We explained to him that he had been charged with being a war criminal and that we had been appointed by the American Army to defend him. He was entitled to any lawyers he wanted, we said—he might even send to Japan for counsel if he did not wish to avail himself of our services. Yamashita smiled. 'I am very grateful to the United States government for furnishing me counsel,' he replied. 'I appreciate your giving up time from what must be pressing duties to defend me.'"

The lawyers briefly informed their new client of the general nature of the charges that would be filed against him. Basically, the prosecution would say that he had violated the articles of war by failing to control his troops, allowing them to engage in innumerable acts of brutality. Yamashita asked the lawyers for details: Where were the atrocities committed? By whom? When?

The lawyers shook their heads. At the arraignment they would ask the commission for a "bill of particulars," a detailed description of each of the charges. For now, all they had were vague generalities. However, they included allegations of rape, torture, murder, mistreatment of prisoners, and the destruction of Manila. Did Yamashita know about any of these matters?

The general was adamant; he had never heard of any of these things. Had he discovered them, he assured the lawyers, he would have had those responsible punished. And if, in fact, these crimes had really taken place . . .

The lawyers interrupted him. There was no question about it, they informed him. The atrocities had taken place; they were proven fact.

One of the lawyers pressed Yamashita. It was important, he explained to his client, that his attorneys know the full truth. A defense was more effectively constructed if the lawyers knew what to expect from the forthcoming evidence. The general would be protected by the attorney-client privilege, he said, but it was imperative to the defense of the case to know just what Yamashita's involvement had been.

Yamashita nodded his head slowly.

Then Captain Reel asked the critical question, the question on the minds of each of the lawyers: How could so many atrocities have been committed in Manila without the general knowing about them?

Yamashita's lengthy reply, Reel later wrote, was

> the story of a man with a mission to perform, a man who was beset by overwhelming difficulties and harrassed by overpowering forces, a man who was entirely unable to carry out the ordinary functions of a desk commander in a rear echelon, whose ability to communicate with his troops was destroyed, and who was finally isolated and crushed by the superior power of his opponents. . . .
>
> Thus we saw revealed tha picture of Yamashita's insurmountable difficulties upon his arrival in the islands, the blueprint of a situation that began with such a welter of impossible tasks that there simply was no time for training procedures or even inspection trips and that ended with the general's virtual isolation from the diverse elements of a scattered command. The state of his communications was

such that he could not know of atrocities which we
said Japanese troops had committed . . .

The courtroom for the trial was in reality the ornate
reception hall of the high commissioner's residence in
Manila. Toward the front of the great hall was a slightly
raised platform, with a long table and five leather swivel
chairs; this was the judge's bench. Behind the chairs, the
baroque wall wrapped around the stage in a graceful arc,
with seven French doors offering a panoramic view of
Manila Bay. Between the two windows directly behind
the center chair—reserved for the president of the Commission, General Reynolds—were two staffs bearing flags
with the emblems of the United States and the Philippines. To the right of the judge's bench were a table and
chairs for the prosecution; to the left, the defense counsel's table. Directly in front of the bench were two chairs,
one for the official interpreter and one for the court reporter. Further in front of the bench, and between the
opposing counsel tables, a single wooden chair sat on
another raised platform—the witness seat.

Microphones seemed to be everywhere—on the tables,
in various positions on the bench, next to the interpreter,
beside the witness chair—and were connected by a complex mass of tangled black electrical cords. Loudspeakers
hung from the elaborate designs of the ceiling and jutted
out from behind ornate decorations along the walls. In
the wings on either side of the hall, leading to connecting
rooms, were large mounted spotlights; from the ceiling,
six high-intensity klieg lights were suspended, designed
to aid the motion-picture cameramen as they filmed the
trial. And to accommodate the many spectators, 300 seats
had been arranged in orderly rows along the back area of
the great hall. The first two rows were reserved for generals on the left, newspaper reporters on the right; photographers were permitted to roam freely, taking flash

pictures throughout the trial. The remaining rows of seats were given out to the public on a first-come, first-served basis. And there was no shortage of spectators; the audience was packed for the entire six weeks of trial with the angry citizens of Manila, anxious to see the Jap mass murderer pay for his crimes.

On October 8, 1945, Yamashita rose from his chair behind the defense table and stood in respectful silence during his pretrial inquest. Across the room from him, Major Kerr began reading from a many-paged document. The great hall, packed now to overflowing, was silent; everyone was studying the bald, bull-necked general, getting their first look at the legendary "Tiger of Malaya."

"Tomoyuki Yamashita," Kerr read, "General, Imperial Japanese Army, between 9th October 1944 and 2nd September 1945, at Manila and other places in the Philippine Islands, while commander of armed forces of Japan at war with the United States of America and its allies, unlawfully disregarded and failed to discharge his duty as commander to control the operations of the members of his command, permitting them to commit brutal atrocities and other high crimes against the people of the United States and of its allies and dependencies, particularly the Philippines, and he, General Tomoyuki Yamashita, thereby violated the laws of war."

Yamashita remained silent as Colonel Clarke stood and asked that before entering a plea of "not guilty," the defense be supplied with a bill of particulars describing the crimes in more detail. Failed to discharge what duty? when? where? failed to control what "operations of the members of his command"? permitted them to commit what "brutal atrocities"? when and where was the permission given? and what was meant by "and other high crimes"?

Surprisingly, Kerr objected to Clarke's request for a more specific charge. It might be "appropriate in a court

of law," he said, "but certainly not in this proceeding."
The defense had no procedural right to know what the
exact charges were against him!

Finally, Kerr agreed to supply a list of sixty-four specific charges which he had in his hand, on the condition
that further charges could be filed later. The commission
agreed, and the list was handed to Clarke. But the cost
was soon to be felt. In return for this seemingly elementary right, Kerr would have the right to file additional
charges at a later date.

Yamashita entered the plea of "not guilty." Quickly
Reynolds set the trial date as requested by the prosecution: October 29, three weeks away. Then, dressed in the
least shabby uniform he had been able to find, Yamashita
walked out of the courtroom with his head erect.

Lieutenant Colonel Meek, chief of the Manila branch of
the war-crimes office, called Clarke that evening. "Damn
it, it makes me mad," he said. "If I had my way I
wouldn't let Yamashita come into court all decked out in
a uniform. Why, goddamit, he stole the show! He domi-
nated the courtroom! If I had my way, I'd put him in
prison overalls and put chains on him. It made me so
mad I wanted to punch him and all of you in the face."

But as Reel noted, "What Meek could not know, or
would not see, was that in this instance clothes did not
make the man. Whatever else might be thought of him,
General Yamashita personified dignity and serenity. Vic-
tor or vanquished, commander or captive, he carried
himself like a man."

The defense lawyers worked frantically during the
three weeks remaining before the trial, trying desperately to locate witnesses and investigate the facts behind
the sixty-four separate instances of misconduct charged
by the prosecution. But it was a hopeless task from the
beginning. "All we could do was to go over each of the
particulars with Yamashita and his staff officers," Reel

later recalled, "learn from them who might be in a position to know what had happened, interview those prisoners, satisfy ourselves that the General did not know of the occurrences, that his communications at the time and place involved were such that he could not know of them, perhaps that the troops that were at the particular location at the moment were not then under his command."

Then, two days before trial was to begin, a messenger arrived at Colonel Clarke's office with an envelope. Inside the envelope was another bill of particulars, outlining fifty-nine new charges against Yamashita. "We were dumbfounded," Reel was later to write. "We had expected that perhaps one or two or three new items might be added. But here we were, just two days before trial, and the charges that we would have to meet were almost doubled—from 64 to 123, and practically all of them involving new places, new persons, new witnesses."

On the following day, the lawyers did the only thing they could—they appeared before the commission and requested a continuance. Reel pointed out to the court that even MacArthur's own rules for the trial clearly stated, "The accused shall be entitled to have in advance of trial a copy of the charges and specifications, so worded as clearly to apprise the accused of each offense charged."

Reel then continued, pleading to the generals for time to prepare a defense. "We earnestly state that we must have this time in order to prepare a defense adequately. I might add, sir, we think that this is important to the accused, but far more important than any rights of this accused, we believe, is the proposition that this commission should not deviate from a fundamental American concept of fairness, decency, and justice, which dictates that an accused has a right to defend himself."

The commission was unmoved. "The motion of defense counsel for a continuance is not sustained," General Reynolds said calmly.

It was not until later that the defense lawyers were accidentally to stumble over a radiogram that was to explain the unseemly speed with which Yamashita was being tried. The radiogram was addressed to the war-crimes branch office in Manila and bore the return address of General MacArthur's headquarters in Tokyo. The message was simple and to the point: MacArthur was "disturbed at reports of a possible continuance" in the Yamashita case; he "doubted the need of defense for more time," and "urged" haste.

And so, on October 29, the trial began in the case of the *United States of America versus Tomoyuki Yamashita.*

"The commission, no doubt, is aware of the fact that General MacArthur's regulations governing the trial of war crimes establish extremely broad discretionary powers to the commission, as to the receipt of evidence, as to the form of the evidence which it will admit, and generally as to its procedural policies." Major Kerr paused in his opening statement for a moment, looking at each of the generals on the tribunal.

"Furthermore, sir, the Articles of War do not apply to this commission in any particular. It is so ruled by the Judge Advocate General, and if the commission or the defense so desires, I will be glad to supply a copy of that recent ruling. The Articles of War are not binding upon, do not apply to this commission. This commission, sir, is not a judicial body: it is an executive tribunal set up by the Commander-in-Chief." Again, he paused, then continued.

"We are cognizant of the commission's desire that this proceeding be expedited as much as possible. That, likewise, is our desire. Military justice, we realize, is expeditious; it brooks of no unreasonable delays. It does not tolerate the tortuous technicalities which characterize criminal procedure in the law courts of the States. We are proceeding upon that basis."

Yamashita's lawyers looked at each other in stunned disbelief. Here, in his opening statement to the military tribunal, the prosecutor was laying down terms to the generals. Rather than just summarizing the nature of the evidence that will be produced, which is the purpose of an opening statement, he was telling the generals how they were to conduct the trial!

In essence, the prosecutor was telling, not suggesting to, the commission that they could ignore all normal rules of evidence and procedure, and do whatever they wished. Further, he was telling them that they were not even a judicial body and reminding them that MacArthur had put them there. On top of this, he was boldly claiming that the protections of the Articles of War had been somehow suspended! The very articles which Yamashita was charged with violating, were now said not to apply so as to protect his rights. And finally, in an unbelievable statement, Kerr was telling the generals that the trial should be "expedited"—conducted and finished as quickly as possible, with no "technicalities" such as due process slowing down the job.

The conduct of the defense during the trial now became the job of Captain Reel, Captain Sandberg, and Colonel Clarke. Lieutenant Colonel Feldhaus was in the hospital, Major Guy was in Japan interviewing character witnesses, and Lieutenant Colonel Hendrix was buried in legal research. Overwhelmed, the three men fought back from day to day, trying to deal with the flood of evidence that was being introduced.

Yet the result was never really in doubt. As the reporter from *Newsweek* magazine observed, "In the opinion of probably every correspondent covering the trial, the military commission came into the courtroom the first day with the decision already in its collective pocket."

Witness after witness paraded through the courtroom, telling unbelievable stories of horror and sadism. A Filipino woman testified: "I had two children, one on each hand. We were near the river and the Japanese was dragging my child away from me. When I looked over at my girl child, I saw that she was bayoneted right on the breast which penetrated through the back. I was bayoneted on my back five times. My two children were killed." As she left the stand, the woman shook her fist at Yamashita, screaming, "Tandaan mo! Yamashita!" (*Remember it! Yamashita!*)

An old man testified: "My three Chinese friends were kneeling before a ditch the Japanese soldiers had made them dig. The soldiers advanced with fixed bayonets and thrust the bayonets into the bodies of the kneeling Chinese. Then they kicked the bodies into a ditch. About five yards away from us, I saw a Japanese officer with a big sabre in his hands. He went forward and lifted his sword and cut off the head of a Chinese."

And so it went for witness after witness. A seemingly unending series of brutal atrocities was laid out for the commission and for the restive Filipino audience. The spotlights shone, the cameras rolled on, flash bulbs popped.

Every type of evidence submitted by the prosecution was accepted by the commission. The majority of the case consisted of affidavits, testimony immune from cross-examination. "Almost anything passed for evidence," the *Newsweek* reporter observed, "even third-hand hearsay."

Not once during the entire eight days of the prosecution's presentation was there a single shred of credible evidence linking Yamashita to the atrocities. There was no credible witness or document to establish that he had ordered any of the action, been present during any of the atrocities, or even known of the existence of the incidents. The prosecution's case consisted almost entirely of parading victims of the brutalities; Yamashita's involvement was totally ignored.

Even the reporters covering the trial—all initially sympathetic to the prosecution's cause—began to reflect disgust at the proceedings. After the third day, for example, the correspondent for the London *Daily Express*, Henry Keyes, forwarded the following dispatch to his paper:

> Yamashita trial continued today—but it isn't a trial. I doubt that it is even a hearing. Yesterday his name was mentioned once. Today it was not brought up at all. The Military Commission sitting in judgement continued to act as if it wasn't bound by any law or rules of evidence. I hold no brief for any Jap, but in no British court of law would accused have received such rough treatment as Yamashita. The Yamashita trial has been hailed as the most important of the Pacific, not because it is the first, but because the present Commission is supposed to be setting precedents for all future war criminal trials. The trial is supposed to establish that a military commander is responsible for any acts of any of his troops. At the same time, under British law, anyway, he's supposed to have rights. The present Commission pleads saving of time and money, but the facts are so far that Yamashita's American counsel haven't had a hearing.

As the four-week prosecution testimony dragged on, one fact kept reappearing with regular consistency. Witness after witness admitted, under cross-examination, that the Japanese "soldiers" committing the atrocities wore anchors on their caps. And only sailors and marines wore anchors in the Japanese military forces—in this case, the drunken, rampaging sailors and marines of Admiral Iwabuchi's naval force.

When it came time for testimony regarding the failure to feed, clothe, and care for the American prisoners-of-war sufficiently, the story was the same. No evidence was produced to indicate that Yamashita had ordered or condoned any mistreatment. In fact, there was not even any evidence that the articles of the Geneva Convention had been broken—that the Japanese soldiers were receiving any more food, clothing, or medicine than the prisoners.

Yet even those witnesses that were produced were protected from any meaningful cross-examination by the defense. The commission viewed such questioning essentially as a "waste of time." In fact, General Reynolds was to issue an order to the attorneys half-way through the trial: "As a further means of saving time . . . cross-examination must be limited to essentials, and avoid useless repetition of events or opinions. Except in unusual or extremely important matters, the commission will itself determine the credibility of witnesses."

Reel, Sandberg, and Clark did everything they humanly could to present evidence on behalf of General Yamashita. But there was relatively little they could produce. There simply had been no time to locate witnesses; certainly, Iwabuchi and all his men were dead. The only thing that could be done was to attempt to establish the conditions prevailing at the time of the atrocities, Yamashita's lack of control over the men committing them, and his complete lack of knowledge due to his battle-inflicted isolation.

Captain Reel called General Muto to the stand. Through Reel, Muto described for the commission the conditions that prevailed during the retreat from the advancing American forces. He explained the insurmountable problems they faced, the confusion of divided command, the lack of food, the loss of communications, the overwhelming power of the American army and navy. But Reel was dealing with five generals on the commission who were desk men; none of them was familiar with modern battle conditions.

When Muto had finished, Reel produced seven of the most prominent citizens of Japan to testify as to Yamashita's character. They described the high regard with which the general was held in Japan by the common people and his reputation politically as a moderate who had been opposed to warfare and to the powerful Tojo clique. This latter testimony was reinforced by Reel with the submission of numerous U.S. Army intelligence reports. But the defense lawyers knew that the defense rested with the testimony of the final witness: General Yamashita.

The general was at first reluctant to take the witness stand. "What will American people think?" he asked Reel. "In America is it considered proper for a man to testify in his own defense? In Japan it is not done; it is not considered dignified for an accused person to say anything in justification of himself."

In the end, Reel was able to convince him that testifying on his own behalf would not be considered undignified. Reel was convinced that his client would make an excellent impression. And he was right.

Yamashita respectfully answered Reel's questions, described the situation with which he was faced. He explained that he had heard of none of the atrocities until he had come to court; certainly, he had had nothing to do with it.

When Reel was finally finished, Kerr stepped forward. His cross-examination of Yamashita was to last for eleven hours. Yet as Reel later recalled, "In all that time, employing all the craft and skill of the experienced trial lawyer, the chief prosecutor was unable to break down any part of the general's story, to find any inconsistencies, discrepancies or falsehoods in it. Yamashita was in full command of the courtroom during the entire period."

As the questioning wore on, hour after hour, Kerr grew increasingly frustrated. "Do you deny to this commission," Kerr asked angrily, "that you knew of, or ever heard of, any of those killings!"

Yamashita looked squarely at the chief prosecutor. "I never heard of nor did I know of these events."

Kerr jabbed a finger dramatically at the general and shouted, "This is your opportunity to explain to this commission, if you care to do so, how you could have failed to know about those killings!"

Yamashita firmly gripped the arms of the witness chair. He had undergone long hours of examination. He had been thrown in prison, examined by psychiatrists, accused of unknown crimes, rushed through strange proceedings, sat through days of gory testimony. But now he was being yelled at by this major. Quite simply, he had had enough.

With a dignified restraint, Yamashita proceeded to explain in detail the entire circumstances of his retreat from Manila. Calmly, courteously, he described to Kerr and the generals on the commission the conditions with which he was faced. He was through playing question-and-answer games with the clever Major Kerr. And Kerr stood by, helplessly, as Yamashita proceeded to answer his question for forty-two minutes.

> The facts are that I was constantly under attack by large American forces, and I had been under pressure day and night. Under those circumstances, I had to plan, study, and carry out plans of how to combat superior American forces, and it took all my time and effort.
>
> At the time of my arrival, I was unfamiliar with the Philippine situation, and . . . I was confronted with a

superior American force. Another thing was that I was not able to make a personal inspection and to coordinate the units under my command. As a result of the inefficiency of the Japanese system—Japanese army system—it was impossible to unify my command, and my duties were extremely complicated.

Another matter was that troops were scattered about a great deal, and the communications would, of necessity, have to be good; but the Japanese communications were very poor and, therefore, the communications were not all they should have been.

Reorganization of the military force takes quite a while, and these various troops which were not under my command, such as the air force and the Third Maritime Command, were—and the navy—were gradually entering the command one at a time, and it created a very complicated situation. The source of command and coordination within a command is or lies in trusting your subordinate commanders. Under these circumstances, I was forced to confront the superior United States forces with subordinates whom I did not know and with whose character and ability I was unfamiliar. . . .

I tried to dispatch staff officers and various people to the outlying units, but the situation was such that they would be attacked by guerrillas en route and would be cut off. Consequently, it became very difficult to know the situation in these separated groups. And under conditions like this and with both the communication equipment and personnel of low efficiency and old type, we managed to maintain some liaison, but it was gradually cut off, and I found myself completely out of touch with the situation.

I believe that under the foregoing conditions I did the best possible job I could have done. However, due to the above circumstances, my plans and my strength were not sufficient to the situation, and if these things happened, they were absolutely unavoidable. They were beyond anything that I would have expected. If I could have foreseen these things, I would have concentrated all my efforts toward preventing it.

Yamashita finished his explanation, then turned to Kerr. "That's all I have to say."

The commission instructed the lawyers for the defense that they were to have one day to present closing arguments. Sandberg began the summation of the defense by commenting that "no one will ever know the complete story of what happened in Manila in those bloody days of February, 1945. The Japanese who participated cannot tell because undoubtedly they are all dead. But there is one fact which emerges clear and unmistakable from the welter of conflicting reports, rumor and gossip, is that General Yamashita did not want fighting in the city of Manila and that what happened occurred not only against his judgment and his wishes but against his express orders."

Turning to the actual perpetrators of the atrocities—Iwabuchi's sailors and marines—Sandberg continued:

> It is true that they passed to his command on paper, but it is also true that the only important order he gave them—the order to evacuate—they failed to carry out. In addition, even so far as land operations were concerned, General Yamashita's authority was limited to the tactical, the order to advance or retreat. Over supply, personnel, billeting and—most important—discipline, he had no control.
>
> But most important of all is the practical problem. How can the man possibly be held accountable for the action of troops which passed into his command only one month before, at a time when he was 150 miles away—troops which he had never seen, trained or inspected, and over whose actions he has only the most nominal control?
>
> The prosecution contends that there is a problem in the Manila atrocities. We do not see any. We see only wild, unaccountable looting, murder and rape. If there be an explanation of the Manila story, we believe it lies in this: trapped in the doomed city,

> knowing that they had only a few days at best to
> live, the Japanese went berserk, unloosed their pent-
> up fears and passions in one last orgy of abandon.

Finished, Sandberg sat down. Reel rose now and addressed the panel of generals. He too reviewed the evidence that had been presented by the prosecution and
reminded the tribunal of the impossible situation with
which Yamashita had been faced. Finally, he concluded
his arguments. "General Yamashita's problem was not
easy. Harrassed by American troops, by our Air Forces,
by the guerrillas, even by conflicting and unreasonable
demands of his superiors, he was on the run from the
moment he got here. . . . Of course, he did not have time
to inspect prisoners. When we judge him, sir, we must
put ourselves in his place, and I say that, unless we are
ready to plead guilty before the world to a charge of
hypocrisy, to a charge that we supinely succumbed to the
mob's desire for revenge, then we must find General
Yamashita not guilty of these charges!"

It was now the prosecution's turn. Major Kerr stood
from behind his table and walked to the middle of the
great hall. "Under laws generally," he began, "any man
who, having the control of the operation of a dangerous
instrumentality, fails to exercise that degree of care which
under the circumstances should be exercised to protect
third persons is responsible for the consequences of his
dereliction of duty. We say, apply that in this case! Apply
that in the field of military law!"

Unfortunately for Major Kerr, there was no such principle in military law. He was telling the commission to apply
to the military situation a principle of negligence from
American civil law. Yamashita had shown "negligence,"
Kerr continued, and "that may be manslaughter."

Kerr then carried his almost unbelievable theory to a

ridiculous extreme, citing as his sole legal precedent for
executing Yamashita an old Connecticut case:

> I have in mind the case of the burning of the circus
> tent, I believe in Connecticut, a few years ago. Of-
> ficers and employees of the circus company were
> charged and, I am informed, convicted of criminal
> charges and sentenced to prison terms. Not because
> they ordered that the circus tent be burned, not be-
> cause they ordered that the innocent, helpless wom-
> en and children there be killed, but because they
> failed to take action which, if taken, would have pre-
> vented the catastrophe. They had failed to take the
> steps which, if taken, would have prevented the trag-
> edy; it was foreseeable, and they were charged with
> having had knowledge that, if they failed to take
> those ultimate precautions, this thing might have
> happened. We say the same thing of Yamashita.

Incredible as it may seem, the prosecution was attempting to legally justify a war-crimes conviction on the
basis of an old Connecticut negligence-manslaughter
case. It would have been laughable were it not that
Yamashita's life hung on the decisions of five men totally
unfamiliar with Connecticut or any other law. And Kerr
did not ask for a manslaughter verdict. Concluding his
arguments later, he said, "We recommend that the sentence be death—carried out by hanging."

With arguments concluded, General Reynolds thanked
the lawyers and court personnel for cooperating with the
commission in conducting the trial "with dispatch." Ad-
journing the trial, he said, "The commission will announce its findings at two o'clock in the afternoon, Friday next."

The fate of General Yamashita hung now on the wis-
dom of those five generals.

On Friday, December 7, 1945, on the fourth anniver-
sary of the Japanese attack on Pearl Harbor, the trial pro-

ceedings in the matter of the United States vs. Yamashita resumed.

While waiting for the commission to return to the courtroom with a decision, the newspaper reporters milled around discussing the possible verdicts. Although there were over fifty reporters there to hear what the verdict would be, only twelve of them—American, British, and Australian—had covered the entire trial from the beginning. The fact that twelve of them had heard all of the evidence struck Pat Robinson, the correspondent for the International News Service. He polled the twelve-man "jury" in a secret ballot: Was Yamashita guilty? The vote was 12 to 0: No.

The courtroom was called to order. Before the commission took the bench, the chief of the military police guards, Major Jack Kenworthy, addressed the courtroom: "There will be no demonstrations," he said. "When the judgment is pronounced, you will not utter any sound or make any display, either of pleasure or of dissatisfaction." Then Kenworthy, who had been present at Yamashita's surrender and who had guarded him for the past three months, walked over to the general's interpreter and whispered in his ear: "Tell General Yamashita that no matter what the court says, I'll always think of him as a great guy—and as a real gentleman."

At two o'clock, the five generals entered the great hall and took their places on the bench. Quickly, General Reynolds read a prepared statement setting forth the charges and summarizing the evidence. Then he ordered Yamashita, Clarke, and the interpreter to stand in front of him. Were there any statements General Yamashita wished to make before the judgment of the court were rendered? Yamashita nodded.

> I have been arraigned and tried before this honorable commission as a war criminal. I wish to state

that I stand here today with the same clear conscience as on the first day of my arraignment, and I
swear before my Creator and everything sacred to
me that I am innocent of the charges made against
me.

With reference to the trial itself, I wish to take this
opportunity to express my gratitude to the United
States of America for having accorded to an enemy
general the unstinted services of a staff of brilliant,
conscientious, and upright American officers and
gentlemen as defense counsel.

General Reynolds nodded, then resumed reading from
the papers in front of him.

General Yamashita: The commission concludes: (1)
That a series of atrocities and other high crimes have
been committed by members of the Japanese armed
forces under your command against the people of
the United States, their allies, and dependencies
throughout the Philippine Islands; that they were
not sporadic in nature but in many cases were methodically supervised by Japanese officers and noncommissioned officers; (2) that during the period in
question you failed to provide effective control of
your troops as was required by the circumstances.

Accordingly, upon secret written ballot, twothirds or more of the members concurring, the commission finds you guilty as charged and sentences
you to death by hanging.

9
U.S.A. v. Homma

GENERAL MASAHARU HOMMA WAS TAKEN FROM TOKYO to a prisoner-of-war camp outside the city, where he was held incommunicado for questioning by the prosecution. On October 18, Major General Yoshio Nasu, representing the Military Affairs Board to the Japanese War Ministry, paid him a brief visit. Visibly embarrassed, he informed Homma that the decision had been made to strip him of his rank and honors for a period of one year.

Homma was stunned. After recovering from the initial shock, he asked Nasu why this had been done. Nasu explained that the new Japanese government wanted to help Homma and that by taking this action they would be temporarily disassociating themselves from him—thus permitting them to take part in the trial. The government incorrectly believed that MacArthur would appoint a joint American-Japanese tribunal to try the war criminals.

On December 8, Homma was transferred to the prison

facility at Sugamo. There, his uniform and decorations were taken from him, and, a few days later, he was transported to Manila, dressed now in a dull grey civilian suit. There was to be no commanding presence of a handsomely uniformed general in this trial, as there had been in Yamashita's.

At the prisoner-of-war camp in Los Baños, a few miles from Manila, Homma continued politely answering the questions thrown at him by the psychiatrists, investigators, and prosecutors. As before, the prosecution team had long since been appointed from the experienced ranks of MacArthur's legal staff. Led by the chief prosecutor, Lieutenant Colonel Frank E. Meek, they had been busy during the previous months gathering evidence to be used against Homma. Assisting Meek was Major Manuel Lim of the Philippine Army's Judge Advocate General's staff, Captain Delmas Hill, and Lieutenants Paul White, Abram Riff, and Benjamin Schwartz. Schwartz, a particularly skilled prosecutor, had been specially transferred from the navy for the sole purpose of working on the Homma case.

After the prosecution was through with General Homma, they turned him over to his newly appointed defense lawyers. The trial was only four short weeks away when he first met the American officers who had hastily been drafted and thrown together to defend him: Major John Skeen, Captain George Furness, Captain Frank Coder, and Captain George Ott. Skeen was named chief counsel, and he was to assume the lion's share of the trial responsibilities. Of the four lawyers, only Ott was from the Judge Advocate's office; Skeen was in the infantry, Coder in field artillery, and Furness in the air corps.

As if in a replay of the Yamashita script, Skeen and his small staff found themselves scrambling frantically to investigate the facts and put together evidence in time for the date scheduled for the beginning of the trial: January

8, 1946. And as had Yamashita's lawyers, they quickly realized the absurd impossibility of the task.

Meanwhile, MacArthur once again named five generals to sit on the commission. The only difference in this commission was that a Filipino had been included—Major General Basilio J. Valdez of the Philippine Army. Brigadier Generals Robert A. Gard, Warren M. McNaught, and Arthur G. Trudeau were added to the commission. The presiding judge's position was filled by Major General Leo Donovan, the same General Donovan who had just taken part in the conviction of General Yamashita.

On December 18, Homma was brought before the new commission for arraignment. Again, the trial setting was the great hall of the high commissioner's residence in Manila. And as with General Yamashita, the proceedings were to be conducted in an atmosphere of spotlights, motion-picture cameras, popping flashbulbs, milling reporters, and a packed audience of hostile Filipinos. The show was the same; only the characters had been changed.

Before reciting the charges, Meek advised the commission that the proceeding was not to be a strictly judicial one. Reading from MacArthur's orders, he reminded them, "The commission shall apply the rules of evidence and pleadings set forth herein with the greatest liberality to achieve expeditious procedure." He then also reminded them that the ultimate decision as to innocence or guilt and as to sentence would not be "carried into effect until approved by the officer who convened the commission. . . . Such officer shall have authority to approve, mitigate, remit in whole or in part, commute, suspend, reduce or otherwise alter the sentence imposed, or remand the case for rehearing before a new commission." In other words, MacArthur could almost completely ignore the decision of this commission, should he not like their verdict!

Meek then turned to Skeen and Homma, seated behind the defense table, and handed them a list of forty-seven allegations of war crimes. The accusatory list charged that Homma was responsible for numerous atrocities committed during the Death March, that he had violated the "open city" status of Manila in shelling it after MacArthur's withdrawal, that prisoners of war had been mistreated in the camps, and that isolated instances of brutality had been committed by Japanese soldiers against Filipinos in the field.

Skeen accepted the list of accusations, then requested the commission to require the prosecution to be more specific in its charges; because of the vagueness of most of the counts, it was difficult to know exactly when and where the alleged atrocities had taken place and by whom they had been committed. The request was preemptorily denied and a plea of "not guilty" was entered.

Skeen then advised the generals that, as the defense counsel had just been appointed, there was insufficient time within which to investigate adequately the forty-seven separate charges and prepare a defense. "Now," Skeen continued,

> this is based on the fact that these charges, the dates in which they occurred, are three years ago. The Defendant has great difficulty remembering specific instances and persons that might prove helpful; 75 percent of the possible witnesses are at present in Japan, and some are in Korea, and some in China.
>
> For that reason, sir, in all fairness and justice to the Accused, and in addition the fact that the defense has just taken over this case a few days ago, we feel that a [delay] is not at all an unreasonable request.

General Donovan looked sternly at Skeen. "Do you have anything else?"

"No, sir," Skeen replied.

Donovan then promptly denied the request. "The commission will now recess and reconvene on the 3rd of January, 1946 . . ."

Perhaps surprised at the denial, Skeen interrupted Donovan. "May I say something else, sir?"

"Yes," Donovan replied curtly.

"It's a question of . . . the tremendous amount of research and the tremendous amount of people that must be interviewed before we can even start."

"I understand that," Donovan said. "The commission will now be in recess and reconvene on the 3rd of January."

On January 3, 1946, the trial of General Masaharu Homma began. It was to continue uninterrupted for one month, in many ways indistinguishable in character or format from Yamashita's trial.

As Kerr had done, Meek's case was to consist almost entirely of parading the victims of terrible atrocities through the courtroom, recounting their agonizing experiences, and showing the generals their gruesome scars. And again, the presence of any credible evidence pointing to Homma's ordering any of the atrocities, or to even knowing of their existence, was totally absent; again, the prosecution was proceeding on a vague theory of negligence. Skeen had requested that the prosecution specify exactly what that theory was. He asked the commission for a "bill of particulars" setting forth: "(a) What duties of a commander-in-chief in the Philippines of the armed forces of Japan he is charged with disregarding or failing to discharge; (b) How and in what manner he disregarded or failed to discharge the duties referred to; (c) What measures for the control over members of his command he should have taken and is charged with disregarding or failing to take." In other words, Homma's

lawyers insisted on at least knowing what was meant by
the negligence theory: what was the standard which he
had violated, and how? The commission, however, refused to comply with even this simple and obvious request. Homma would be tried, as had been Yamashita,
on the basis of an unprecedented negligence theory that
had never been described or even recognized before.

The commission quickly turned to the presentation of
evidence. And throughout the trial, there was to be a
sense of urgency, a seemingly pressing need to quickly
conclude the formality of the trial and get on with the
sentencing.

Colonel Meek began his case with an opening statement to the commission.

> There is in the possession of the prosecution a great
> mass of evidence of the cruelties, of the starvations,
> of the tortures, the most cold-blooded murders
> under the most sadistic conditions, the barbarous,
> brutal, unparalleled, cruel and needless conditions
> under which the Death Marches were conducted,
> the lack of food, clothing, medical supplies, as well
> as the tortures, the starvations and the murders in
> the internment and prisoner-of-war camps, to pre-
> sent all of which would occupy many months. . . .
> We will show conclusively that these atrocities were
> committed by the forces under the command of this
> Accused; that they were so widespread and so broad
> in pattern and design and so continuous that they
> will lead to the one and final conclusion that they
> were within the knowledge of this Accused, *or that
> they should have been* . . . [italics added]

Once again, the prosecution would not—could not—
prove that Homma knew of any of the atrocities. Once
again, the prosecution would ask for his execution because he *should* have known.

Meek then briefly discussed the additional charges—

violation of an open city and the refusal to accept Wainwright's surrender. Of course, these were ridiculous charges to begin with. As the U.S. Army's Chief of Military History has since admitted, Manila was, in fact, not an open city; MacArthur still kept troops in it, and both he and Homma knew it. Similarly, Wainwright later admitted having lied to Homma about his authority at the initial surrender negotiations; Homma knew of the deceit and was absolutely correct in refusing to accept a surrender of anything less than Wainwright's complete command. It was, therefore, the Death March and the prison camps that became the focus of attention.

The testimony concerning the prisoner-of-war camps proved a big disappointment to the prosecution. Over and over, witnesses testified that the treatment they received and the conditions they lived under actually worsened from the first months of their internment as the war ground on. And one unavoidable fact remained, perhaps unknown to Meek and his staff: Homma was recalled permanently to Japan only one month after the Corregidor campaign had been successfully completed. MacArthur's army on Bataan surrendered in early April and began the Death March to the prisoner-of-war camps soon thereafter; yet from that date until Wainwright's surrender on May 8th, Homma was totally preoccupied many miles away with the campaign against the almost impregnable fortress on Corregidor, justifiably leaving subordinates in command of the prison camps. And during the one-month period following Corregidor's fall, he was busy in "mop-up" skirmishes around the islands, arranging for General Sharp's surrender, engaging in guerrilla operations, occupying the Philippines, establishing an administration to govern the country, dealing with a hostile headquarters in Tokyo, and handling literally hundreds of other important matters. It would have been unrealistic to have expected any commanding general personally to supervise the prisoner-of-war camps during this busy one-month period; certainly, it is doubtful whether MacArthur personally reviewed the running of prison camps in Japan and the Philippines in the month following Japan's surrender.

Nevertheless, Meek continued in efforts to brand Homma with responsibility for the conditions in the camps. Witness after witness testified to the shortage of food and medicine and to the poor facilities supplied: *We had six showers and six toilets and two wash basins. There was a long line every minute of the day. . . . We used to have water at certain parts of the day, and then it would go off. . . . On the second floor the water wouldn't go up that high, and we had to go down to the first floor. . . . We never got a private shower, all through the internment; I don't think I ever bathed alone. . . . The mosquitos were terrible, the place was filthy. . . . The medical facilities were very poor. . . . The Japanese doctors would come into our hospital occasionally; mostly, we had to depend on our own doctors. . . . Our doctors had to go to nearby civilian hospitals to operate on our men because we didn't have proper facilities. . . . Approximately 100 men died the first year.*

Evidence of individual instances of brutality was produced: *They were dragged into a room as far as I could see, they had a rope, beating them. There were two men doing the beating, strangers in the camp. . . . The three men were dragged to a grave prepared, according to my understanding, in the Japanese fashion. From a position about 15 to 20 feet distant, three M.P.'s lined up, and with their service revolvers fired a shot at each of these men. They collapsed and fell into the grave. They were charged with escape.*

Periodically, the prosecution would attempt to narrow the time range down to the period before Homma was recalled to Japan. Invariably, however, this backfired: The deaths or physical mistreatments usually had taken place after Homma had gone.

Meek returned to the parade of brutalities:

I was taken up, tied up, trussed up like a chicken, held up by two Japanese soldiers while another one started slapping me on both sides of the face with both hands, so that the ends of the fingers would slap me on the temple. And they started beating me up and beating me until I collapsed. Then they used to revive me, put me up again, give me the same treatment. . . . A certain Sergeant Imai took some kind of a blackjack, cleverly made of a steel coil with a big lump of lead at the end, and he beat me with that for about 15 minutes until I collapsed. . . . They got hold of my hand and started asking questions, and as I wouldn't answer they pulled up the thumb till it snapped. . . . I used to hear women screaming and asking for mercy in the neighborhood cells. They told me, "You better confess because that is your three daughters and your wife hanging naked from the roof."

With sickening regularity, the witnesses took the stand and recounted their horror stories. But as the days passed, one thing became very clear—the name of Masaharu Homma was not being mentioned. Among all of the witnesses who were to testify to atrocities they had seen committed, not a single one mentioned Homma, nor did the prosecution even bother to ask. It was apparently enough to disgust the commission, the press, and the Filipino audience with the horrifying nature of the isolated instances of brutality. The emotional outrage would then demand that someone be made to pay, and Homma would be available, formally charged by lawful authority.

The procession of witnesses continued: "I was blindfolded, forced to kneel on rods, small rods, possibly a half or three-quarters of an inch in diameter. Three of them were placed under my shins, with my feet under me. I was then given a very heavy object to hold over my head and with fiendish cries the beatings started. The beating lasted through most of the night." And another: "I have seen him prostrate on the floor, sopping wet, after having received what was called the 'water cure.' I have heard him cry out in the most agonizing cries that I have ever heard a human being utter." And yet another: "I was asked to lay down on the table with my legs hanging, tied together with my arms tied lightly around my body, and then they placed a towel on my mouth and nose and continually pouring water on this towel until you could hardly breathe and you almost drowned yourself."

Usually, the instances of torture involved interrogations by members of a Gestapo-like organization of military policemen called the *kempeitai*, which operated beyond the control of General Homma, answering only to Tojo and his staff. Yet the torture testimony certainly proved among the most livid and stomach-wrenching of the trial.

Eventually, Meek and his assistants decided that enough had been done on the prisoner-of-war camps. It was time now to direct attention to the primary purpose of the trials, the infamous Death March.

"They lined us up, told us to sit down, to sit down on the ground and stay there."

"Then what happened, Sergeant?" Meek asked.

"Then they told us to march to Mariveles."

"And you went to Mariveles, is that correct?"

"That is right."

"How long did you stay there?"

"Overnight."

"The following morning, did you leave Mariveles?"

"Yes, sir."

"Now, did you see anything out of the ordinary in Mariveles?"

"About eight or nine American boys were found dead along the line."

"Could you tell from looking at these bodies how these men had died?"

"Stabbed from all directions: through the heart, the head, anyplace else. And it was not dying on the battle-field, either."

"What time did you leave, and in what direction did you go?"

"We left about 8:30 in the morning, went up to Little Baguio."

"How many were in the group with you that left?"

"About 150 men or more."

"How long did you stay at Little Baguio?"

"Just about a short time, that is all; a couple of hours, half an hour, an hour or so."

"And how far did you go that day?"

"Cabcaben."

"Now," Meek continued, "between Little Baguio and Cabcaben, did anything occur with respect to your group and the Japanese?"

"Lots of Americans got beaten up by the Japanese."

"Now, did anything occur while you were at Cabcaben on that date?"

"It was night, sir. Corregidor guns were shelling our place there; quite a few Americans were wounded by shelling."

"When did you leave Cabcaben?"

"In the morning, sir, at 12:00."

"How far did you march that day?"

"We went as far as Lamao, and then to Limay."

"Did you stop any place that night?"

"Up to Lamao there was shelling that night. We don't do no stopping there. We stopped at Limay."

"Did anything occur that day on the march from Cab-caben to Limay?"

"Many things. Buddies and lots of Americans and Fili-pinos, and women and men are dying on the left side of the road, many of them."

"Now, when you say 'lots,' can you estimate approximately the number of bodies you saw?"

"I saw at least over 200 Americans," the sergeant replied.

"Could you tell from those bodies how they had been killed?"

"About 75 percent were stabbed by the Japanese bayonets or rifles, or something, and the other fellows were shot to death."

"How long did you remain at Limay?"

"About two hours, I believe."

"Then where did you go?"

"To Orion, then on to Pilar."

"Where did you go from there?"

"Up to Balanga."

"So you left Cabcaben in the morning, and now you are in Balanga is that correct?"

"Yes, sir."

"How long did you remain in Balanga?"

"Two nights, I believe, and two days, if I am not mistaken."

"Now, between Limay and Balanga, did you see anything unusual taking place with respect to the prisoners marching, and the Japanese guards?"

"Between Limay and Balanga was two American Air Corps men were killed by the Japanese guards in front of my own eyes, and I see them."

"How were they killed?"

"Bayoneted. Right through the heart, one of them, and the other one right through the head."

"Now, what was the condition of the grounds that the men slept on in Balanga?"

"It was just dirt, that is all it was."

"Were there any sanitary facilities provided at Balanga?"

"No sanitation whatsoever."

"Now, from the time that you left Mariveles until the time you reached Balanga, did you receive any food from the Japanese?"

"No, sir," he replied. "No food, no water."

"Did you have any food with you?"

"I had some, but they took it from me."

"Who took it away from you?"

"Japanese guards, sir. Also I had a watch that they took away from me, sir."

"At Balanga, were you supplied with any food?"

"No, sir."

"What was the situation with respect to water?"

"No water at all. We take it out of a ditch. There were little places, some kind of a pool that we took water out of there, very dirty."

"Now, what season of the year was this in the Philippines?"

"The hottest season in the year. The months of April, May and June. Very hot, sir."

"What was the condition, what was the physical condition of the other prisoners and yourself when you were in Balanga?"

"There was plenty of dysentery and malaria and other kinds of diseases; beriberi, I think they call it."

"Now, while you were at Balanga, did you witness an incident with respect to two Filipino soldiers?"

"Two Filipinos was digging their own graves and they buried them alive for cooking rice."

"Will you please describe that a little more fully?"

"There was orders that nobody can cook rice at Balanga."

"Where did the men get the rice?"

"You can buy from the outside; Filipinos sell it themselves, Filipino civilians. When I was at Balanga by myself I went to buy three-quarters of a cup of rice, uncooked rice, but we had no chance to cook that rice.

Some of the Filipinos took a chance to cook that rice, but two of the Filipinos are buried alive."

"Who did this?"

"Japanese guards."

"Now, Sergeant, when did you leave Balanga?"

"Two days later, sir."

"About what time?"

"Two o'clock in the afternoon, sir."

"The Japanese gave you some food when you left there, isn't that right?"

"Right after we left there, yes, sir."

"How far did you hike that day?"

"We hiked all through to the next station, Abucay, and then we hiked on to Samal. And then from Samal, we hiked to Orani and then to Hermosa."

"Did you stop at any of the towns?"

"No, we stopped outside of the towns. Then we went to Lubao, the 16th."

"In other words, Sergeant, you marched continuously from Balanga, commencing about two o'clock in the afternoon on the 14th, to sometime on the 16th when you arrived at Lubao?"

"Yes," the Sergeant answered. "Because any man that tried to go—anyone who tried to stop—he cannot hide or anything. He would be finished."

"Now, did something happen to a Colonel McConnel, who was with you during that part of the march?"

"That is right, sir, before we got to Orani; he was shot to death."

"Describe that."

"On the left side of the road, before we got to Orani, Colonel McConnel went in the direction of a big house. I asked the colonel, 'Where are you going?' He said, 'I have to take the chance to go there.' He said, 'I can't make the hike anymore.' I said, 'What is the reason?' He said, 'My feet hurt me.' I said, 'If you go there you will be shot to death.' He said, 'I have to take that chance!' He was shot right in the back before he got to the house."

"Now, how long did you remain in Lubao, Sergeant?"

"Two days and two nights, until the 18th."

"Now describe the concentration area at Lubao."

"I believe Lubao was one of the worst places I have been in yet. When we went down there about ten o'clock at night they put us in a warehouse about 150 feet square; 4,000 Americans, and on our haunches we had to be all night long, and no water or food or anything else until eight o'clock in the morning."

"Now, what food was provided by the Japanese for the prisoners of war at Lubao while you were there?"

"On the 17th we had a little rice—not much, really—and the 18th we got some more rice—not much, just enough to see we got something to eat, anyhow."

"Were there facilities for securing water by the prisoners?"

"We had one spigot to line up there, and the guards, if you rush, would knock you down with a club, rifle, or anything they got. We used to get a canteen of water daily, no more."

"Now, when did you leave Lubao, Sergeant?"

"The 18th, in the afternoon, two o'clock."

"And how far did you march on that day?"

"Marched to San Fernando."

"Where were you kept in San Fernando?"

"Back of a schoolhouse."

"Did you receive food when you arrived at San Fernando?"

"Yes, sir, we had rice and water three times a day while I was there."

"How long did you stay at San Fernando?"

"From the 18th to the 26th."

"How did it happen that you were able to stay there that long?"

"That is the only place we can get something to eat."

"And the Japanese gave you some rice every day?"

"Yes, sir, about a pound of rice three times a day for each of us."

"Did the Japanese provide any medical facilities of any kind?"

"No medical facilities; no doctors or anybody else around except ourselves, except the prisoners."

"Now, what happened on the 26th of April, 1942?"

"They tell us to move out, we are going to Camp O'Donnell."

"Where did they take you?"

"To Camp O'Donnell, take us to the train first. From the train they take us to Camp O'Donnell."

And so the testimony of the long list of witnesses went on, each telling his story of diseased and dying men being pushed beyond their limits, of helpless prisoners bayoneted or buried alive for little or no reason. And as the atmosphere of the great hall became increasingly permeated with the blood of the Death March, it became ever more difficult for Homma's lawyers to attempt to show that he had not known of the tragic march. Neither the commission nor the restless audience was in any mood to listen to Skeen try to explain that Homma believed he was fighting a force of 30,000 men on Bataan, not 100,000, and that the prisoner-of-war plans were made accordingly. They would not want to listen to Skeen's witnesses testifying that the small group assigned to guarding and transporting the prisoners was simply overwhelmed at the sudden reality of 100,000 men; worse, that the resulting shortage of officers meant many vengeful guards would be unsupervised. They did not want to hear that Homma's own men were also sick and short of food, clothing, and medical supplies.

But Major Skeen had to try.

"Before presenting the case for the defense," Skeen began his opening statement to the commission,

> I wish to set forth certain facts and indicate the basis on which the defense will proceed. Witnesses to these alleged instances are widely scattered, and a thorough investigation of circumstances surrounding some specifications would require many weeks. Japanese witnesses are reluctant to testify for fear of recrimination, and Filipinos for fear of adverse public opinion. However, within the limits of time and personnel available, the defense will show that the Accused, as Commander-in-Chief of the Japanese Imperial Forces in the Philippines, can in no sense be said to have permitted the alleged offenses, since any offenses committed by individual members of the Japanese forces were not with his consent, nor, in fact, known to him.
>
> It will be shown that the Accused has for many years been identified with that minority group of Japanese officers who were opposed to the policies and doctrines of the Imperial Japanese Headquarters in Tokyo; that he has spent many years in England and acquired the reputation in the Japanese Army of possessing independent, moderate, and humanitarian ideas; and that as a result of such reputation the Accused was prevented from holding any policy-making position in the Japanese Army.
>
> It will be shown that the Accused believed in the humane and proper treatment of civilians and prisoners of war as opposed to the severe policy advocated by the Imperial General Headquarters in Tokyo. This fact was made known to staff officers and subordinate unit commanders of the Accused through severe criticism by officers from the Office of the Supreme Chief of Staff of the Imperial Headquarters when on inspection of operations in the Philippines.
>
> As a result of this divergence of opinion between the Accused and the Imperial Headquarters, active

measures were taken by officers of the Imperial Headquarters to interfere with the carrying out of his policies, and vigorous efforts were made to discredit him. The accused was unaware of these activities which circumvented his efforts to maintain discipline and ultimately resulted in his peremptory removal from command.

In fact, Homma had not learned of the insidious Colonel Tsuji's murderous activities until Skeen's hurried investigations and interviews had uncovered the truth.

"It will be shown," Skeen continued,

that as far as the Accused knew, he was well thought of in the Philippines. He was frequently praised by prominent Filipinos for his fairness and justness in civil administration of the Islands.

It will be shown that the Accused issued instructions for the proper treatment of prisoners of war and the civilian population to the troops under his command, both prior to and after the invasion of the Philippines. But it will also be shown that the Accused assumed command of the 14th Army of the Japanese Imperial forces only one month before the invasion of the Philippine Islands. At the time of his assumption of command most of the units comprising the 14th Army were located in Japan, and during the period of command of the Accused, units were continually changing. Under these circumstances it was impossible for any commander to thoroughly indoctrinate his troops with his own policies and ideals.

It must be remembered that during the first five months of his stay in the Philippines, the Accused was engaged in a bitter campaign. Casualties from battle and disease were far above those expected. Supplies of food and medicine were far below requirements. The surrender of Bataan came unexpectedly and added to already great difficulties, the ad-

ditional problems of care and feeding of undernour-
ished and sick war prisoners of a number exceeding
that of his own troops.

Further, the physical condition of American and
Filipino troops was unknown to the Accused until
after the time of surrender. At the same time there
was still before him the assault on an impregnable
fortress which required every available soldier and
all of the limited resources of his army. Under such
circumstances, it was impossible to direct his full
attention to administrative matters, and it became
imperative that the prisoners of war be handled by
the staff on their own initiative and without active
supervision on the part of the Commander-in-Chief.

Skeen looked at the five stony faces seated behind the
bench, then concluded his opening statement.

Upon proof of the above facts, it will appear that the
Accused cannot be held responsible under the charge
in this case in that: first, the Accused never consented, either directly or by implication, to the commission of the atrocities alleged; second, the Accused
never issued any orders which either directed or
could have been construed to permit the commission
of the alleged atrocities; third, the Accused made
every effort and took every precaution that could
have been reasonably expected of any man in his position to insure that such incidents as the alleged
atrocities should not occur.

But Skeen was missing the point: The Yamashita trial
had already proved that the commission did not care
whether Homma condoned the atrocities or even knew of
them. The point was simple—the atrocities had taken
place, and Homma was the commanding officer. While it
was an unheard-of and terribly unjust principle, it was
nevertheless the working premise of the trial.

And so, the defense lawyers called witness after witness, painstakingly establishing in great detail the exact circumstances surrounding the Death March, the conditions concerning the Camp O'Donnell prisoner-of-war camp, the shelling of Manila, and the surrender by Wainwright. But their efforts were futile. The results were a foregone conclusion.

On the evening of January 13, Homma was finally permitted to visit with his beloved wife, Fujiko. It had been the first time he had been allowed to be alone with her since the day he had been arrested returning from Sado Island.

Homma was carrying a lacquered cigarette box and an album of family photographs as he walked into the interview room, gifts she had sent to him while he was in prison. They kissed, held each other for a long moment. Then Homma asked her about the children; they were well, she replied. He nodded silently, then told her that it was too painful to think about the happiness they had enjoyed in the past; it was easier to think of the future.

"I would like my funeral ceremony to be very quiet," he told her, "with only the family present. I shan't need a very large tomb, either."

Fujiko stroked his head. "Masaharu," she said softly, "don't be too depressed. We shall be dining at home again before very long."

Homma shook his head, his eyes filled with resignation. "Things don't look very good. I was amazed to hear the details of Japanese atrocities. Even Major Skeen says that although he is doing his best for me, the case is quite hopeless." He looked down at the lacquered cigarette box, then handed it to his wife.

Quietly, she accepted the box, knowing what would be inside. There were rumors—which were to prove true— that MacArthur would order Homma's body destroyed and scattered, so that the Japanese could never revere his tomb; yet according to Homma's religion, he could not go to heaven without at least part of his body being consecrated at a funeral ceremony. The cigarette box contained two packets of white paper, one holding a lock of Homma's hair and the other clippings of his fingernails. Fujiko was to smuggle these pathetic fragments out of the prison, and later offer them at his funeral rites. These simple remains of his body would free Homma's soul and permit him to join the gods.

Shortly after Fujiko left, Homma sat down and composed a poem for her:

> *Laid down on the altar I am*
> *Offered as a victim to God*
> *For the sake of*
> *My newly born country.*

When the defense had concluded with the percipient witnesses, they then produced character witnesses. Some of the most respected military and governmental leaders came to Manila to testify on behalf of General Homma. When asked to compare Homma and Tojo, for example, one prominent Japanese leader testified:

In the first place, their nature or character was basically different, and two, their ideas and ideologies were totally different; therefore, General Homma was always disliked by General Tojo. In the comparison of their characters, General Homma is a man imbued with high sense—a strong sense of justice. He is a gentle and warm-hearted person, and a man of high character. In contrast to this, Tojo was of very severe nature—is of very severe nature, who tries to push things through recklessly. In the ideological side, General Homma was pro-English. He was a man who believed in peace and is a moderate. He had moderate views in politics and other things. Tojo, on the other hand, is very pro-German and believed in power and authority, and who is an extremist.

One of the most prominent bankers in Manila courageously stepped forward to testify. He noted, "When I first met him I was struck by his quiet and modest attitude. There was no sign of arrogance, in spite of the fact that he was the highest commander of the victorious army, and as I came to know him better I realized that he is really a broad-minded, deep-thinking, sympathetic and considerate individual." When asked if he had ever heard why Homma had been recalled, the banker replied, "I cannot state definitely, but as far as I gathered, the consensus of opinion was that the policy of General Homma towards the Philippine campaign, under his administration, his attitude towards the Philippines, he got too mild and moderate and soft, and he was criticized for that by the extreme circles of the Japanese Army then reigning in Tokyo."

Major General Francis Piggott of the British Army provided further testament:

> I formed a close personal friendship with him. I found him strongly physically and mentally determined, broad-minded and communicative of independent views, humorous and very good company. He was an ardent supporter of Anglo-Japanese alliance; he had no special pro-German proclivities, rather the reverse. . . . Homma visited the front at the beginning of the Chinese War and at his recommendation certain subordinate commanders were removed from command for their responsibility in the Nanking atrocities which occurred after Japanese General Headquarters in China had lost contact with several advanced units.

Finally, the time came to call Homma to the stand. The tall, quiet gentleman strode almost majestically across the hall in his now-baggy civilian suit. Taking the oath, he sat down and began answering the long series of questions. As the witnesses before him had tried to do, Homma attempted to explain to the commission in detail the circumstances surrounding the Bataan incidents. But the situation was difficult to explain to desk officers, and the questioning dragged slowly on. The cross-examination alone was to last for many hours. Not once throughout his testimony was Colonel Meek able to catch Homma in an inconsistency; despite every trick at his command, he was unable to produce any discrepancies.

Finished at last, Skeen had but one remaining witness, Fujiko Homma. General Homma had been adamantly against the lawyers calling his wife and subjecting her to the proceeding, but Skeen had insisted. After hearing and seeing what type of woman she was, the chief defense counsel thought that perhaps the commission just might begin to get an idea of what type of man the general was.

The quietly attractive woman was called and gracefully took her place in the raised witness chair. After a few preliminary questions, Skeen asked her what her husband's ideas were concerning the Japanese Army.

"He said that the military force is a thing which should be used to defend the Motherland, and work in harmony and try to preserve the world peace, and should never be used to invade the other countries. He also said, constantly, that if a country ever engaged in a war of invasion, that country will inevitably lose."

"Was General Homma subjected to criticism for his attitudes?" Skeen asked.

"Yes," she replied politely but firmly. "Because he studied about the United States and England, because he was always interested in the world trends and kept his eyes open on it, and also because he understood Japan thoroughly, he realized that the spread of war was not only a misfortune for Japan but to all mankind. This view was not welcomed and was not popular among the people. People used to call him pro-American, a pro-

American element. At that time that name was an in-sult—an insulting name."

Skeen then stood back from Mrs. Homma. "Can you tell us what kind of man General Homma is?"

Mrs. Homma straightened almost imperceptibly in her chair. "I have come from Tokyo to here and I am proud of the fact that I am the wife of General Homma." She looked directly at her husband, seated ram rod straight behind the defense table, tears welling in his eyes. "I have one daughter, and my wish for her is that some day she will marry a man like my husband, Masaharu Homma."

There were more than a few moist eyes in the audience as the dignified woman sat in the witness chair, her proud bearing somehow highlighted by the confused atmosphere of her surroundings.

That evening General Homma wrote his wife a letter from his prison cell:

> My Dear Fujiko,
>   I was delighted to hear your speech in court today. It was so heroic and showed the Americans and Filipinos what a Japanese lady is really like. They are quite ignorant about us. I think what you did will go down in the history of Japanese women.
>   Though we could not meet every day, the fact that you stayed in Manila has been a great encouragement and consolation to me. I hear you leave this evening for Japan. I shall certainly miss you from tomorrow.
>   Please live on and be happy and healthy. I am deeply sorry I shall never see our children again.
>   I try not to torture myself with thoughts of my execution. But I have prepared myself for it so it does not matter when the last moment comes. I would rather though that it came sooner and suddenly.
>   Your love forever,
>   Masaharu.

On February 9, closing arguments were presented to the commission. Major Skeen once again tried to reason with the generals. "If the commission please, in order to find the Accused guilty under the charge, the prosecution must prove beyond all reasonable doubt that he is connected with the atrocities which have been alleged. The only basis on which the prosecution has sought to prove such vital connection is that these alleged atrocities were so widespread and numerous as to constitute a pattern and design with the result that because of this the Accused must have known of their occurrences. The prosecution admits that had he not known of these incidents he could not be held responsible. . ."

Skeen then continued, summarizing the evidence that had been presented. Finally, he wound up his arguments with a dire warning.

> With no standard by which to determine how many acts within a given period of time constitute a "widespread pattern and design," it is a dangerous precedent to set for posterity to say that in this case such a pattern and design has been established. In the event of our defeat in a future war it is inevitable that the commanding generals of our armies would be accused and tried.
>
> Finally it should be pointed out that all of the evidence is not to be found within the printed pages of the record. In the short space of six weeks all members of his counsel have become thoroughly convinced of the sincerity and integrity of General Homma and are proud to have represented him. . . . You have observed his manner on the witness stand, watched him through these weeks seated at the counsel table while witnesses for and against him testified. Can you say after talking with him that he is a cruel and heartless man that would have permitted his troops to commit atrocities had he known about them?

Should his life be taken, the world will have lost a
man who could do much toward the continuation of
peace.

On February 11, 1946, at 3:00 P.M., the commission
returned a verdict in the case of U.S.A. versus Masaharu
Homma—guilty. The punishment was set at death by
hanging.

10
A Law Unto Itself

The world I knew is now a shameful place.
There will never come a better time
For me to die

THIS WAKA WAS WRITTEN BY GENERAL YAMASHITA IN his cell soon after hearing the sentence of death pronounced upon him by the military commission. As Yamashita finished composing the short poem, Captain Reel, Colonel Clarke, and the other defense lawyers walked up to the steel bars. Yamashita stood and cheerfully greeted the Americans who had fought so valiantly for him throughout the trial. He shook their hands and thanked each of them in turn for the tremendous personal efforts they had made.

Muto, standing behind the lawyers, did not share his commander's gratitude. "Why can't they shoot us like soldiers?" he growled bitterly. Yamashita silenced him with a glance, embarrassed that his chief of staff should display such lack of hospitality to the Americans. Then, smiling, Yamashita began giving away the last few things in life remaining to him. The simple tea set, so important a part of the Japanese sense of tranquility, was presented to one of the lawyers. Good luck coins from China were handed out, as were the hard-won campaign ribbons from his chest. Finally, Yamashita took off his leather belt and handed it to Lieutenant Colonel Hendrix. "You're the only man fat enough to wear this," he laughed and slapped the despondent lawyer on the back to cheer him up.

But Yamashita's lawyers were not yet finished. MacArthur's constant pushing to speed up the trial proceedings had assured that the execution would be scheduled within a few days—leaving insufficient time for an appeal. But the defense team sent an urgent cable to the clerk of the Supreme Court of the United States requesting a stay of the execution until the Court had had the opportunity to read a petition for writ of habeas corpus which was already in the mail.

Two days passed, and the time for Yamashita's hanging drew near. Then the lawyers received word: the secretary of war had stayed the execution pending the appeal to the Philippine Supreme Court.

The members of the commission and the staff of prosecutors were furious when they learned that the verdict had not been automatically accepted. Every procedural obstacle was now thrown in front of the defense lawyers. When a process server was sent by the Philippine Supreme Court to deliver Yamashita's petition to General Styer, the general ran away from him; the court, however, held that the petition had been technically served and set an immediate hearing date.

On November 23, Yamashita's appeal was argued before the court. Lieutenant Colonel Hendrix urged that the commission had been without jurisdiction to try Yamashita; the United States had authority over the Philippines and jurisdiction therefore properly lay in the civil courts.

Hendrix then made an impassioned—and professionally suicidal—speech to the justices of the court.

> We contend that General MacArthur has taken the law into his own hands, is disregarding the laws of the United States and the Constitution, and that he has no authority from Congress or the President. He is a great soldier and general but not a great lawyer. His orders regarding this case are illegal. . . . [The Commission] has violated every law in the world. If you could hear their decisions, you would be shocked and amazed.

This brazen speech from a military officer under MacArthur's direct command caused more than a few eyebrows to raise. The senior defense counsel, Colonel Clarke, wondered aloud whether Hendrix had set himself up for a court-martial by his inflammatory plea. And Yamashita himself appeared worried for the first time since the trial had begun, concerned that the young man had destroyed his own military career in a hopeless cause.

The Philippine Supreme Court finally ruled that Yamashita's petition could not be granted. To do this, the court said in a highly unusual statement, "would be a violation of faith" by interfering with the liberating United States Army.

Again, Yamashita faced an imminent date with the gallows. And again the lawyers sent a cablegram to the clerk of the United States Supreme Court.

GENERAL TOMOYUKI YAMASHITA SENTENCED TO HANG.
IT IS FEARED SENTENCE WILL BE EXECUTED BEFORE
COURT CAN ACT ON PETITION FOR WRIT OF HABEAS COR-
PUS NOW BEFORE COURT AND ON PETITION FOR WRIT
CERTIORARI NOW EN ROUTE TO YOU. WE URGENTLY RE-
QUEST COURT TO ORDER SECRETARY OF WAR TO STAY
EXECUTION UNTIL COURT CAN ACT ON BOTH PETITIONS.

Upon receiving the message, Chief Justice Stone called Solicitor General McGrath, the government's Supreme Court counsel, and suggested that the army stay the execution without the necessity of an order from the Court. Within hours, the Secretary of War radioed MacArthur and advised him to hold off on the execution until the Supreme Court had made a decision. MacArthur flatly refused to put off Yamashita's execution. The Supreme Court had no business with the trial, he said, and he was going to go ahead with the execution! The Secretary then directly ordered MacArthur to postpone the hanging. Reluctantly, MacArthur complied.

On December 20, 1945, the justices of the Supreme Court considered the petition filed on behalf of General Yamashita. After some discussion, the Court set the case down for argument on January 7. Chief Justice Stone specifically requested that three of Yamashita's military lawyers be permitted to fly back to Washington so that the Court could hear their arguments.

Thus, the Supreme Court of the United States had placed squarely before it the case of *General Tomoyuki Yamashita, Petitioner, v. Lieutenant General Wilhelm D. Styer, Respondent*. And with the case came a series of very awkward questions for the Court to consider.

Back in Manila, the lawyers talked among themselves, and it was decided that Captain Reel, Colonel Clarke, and Captain Sandberg would fly to Washington for the arguments; Lieutenant Colonel Hendrix, Major Guy and Lieutenant Feldhaus would remain behind.

Meanwhile, Yamashita was being held in a prisoner-of-war camp on Luzon without the right to have visitors. Muto, however, was still technically considered his counsel and so was able to see him. The two men talked briefly as the Supreme Court date neared. Muto asked his general if there was anything he could do for him back in Japan. Yamashita replied: "Muto, I told you just before I surrendered that I didn't see how I could go back to Japan. I had lost so many men. Once there were 250,000, now more than half are gone. But you remember I said it was my responsibility to see that those remaining men got home all right. Now it must be your responsibility. Take care of them, Muto— see that they get home. That is my last wish. That is my last command." Muto nodded silently.

In Washington, Yamashita's lawyers realized that the Supreme Court would probably address itself only to procedural issues and would be reluctant to look into the evidence brought forth at the trial itself. The Court's primary concern was not to pass judgment on the innocence or guilt of a defendant but to determine whether jurisdictional and constitutional safeguards had been observed. Accordingly, the defense brief limited itself to three basic contentions.

First, the defense argued that the military commission that had been appointed by General Styer at MacArthur's specific command was constituted without lawful authority. The brief recognized that military commissions could be formed for the purpose of trying individuals for war crimes but contended that their jurisdiction ended upon the cessation of hostilities. MacArthur's ability to form the commission had rested upon authorization from the Joint Chiefs of Staff, which in turn depended upon a directive from President Truman. This presidential authority was based upon his broad "war powers." Therefore, the commission's existence depended ultimately upon the validity of the president's exercise of these war powers. But these, the defense asserted, ended with the cessation of hostilities in Japan and the surrender to Mac-Arthur aboard the battleship *Missouri*. Lacking jurisdiction over General Yamashita, the commission's subsequent verdict of guilt and sentence of death were invalid.

This, Yamashita's lawyers realized, was the weakest of the three issues. They therefore concentrated their efforts on the remaining two contentions.

The second area of attack concerned the charges themselves. All of the evidence against Yamashita had been produced to prove isolated instances of misconduct by Japanese soldiers. But Yamashita's culpability rested upon a single accusation—that he had "unlawfully disregarded and failed to discharge his duty as commander to control the operation of the members of his command, permitting them to commit brutal atrocities and other high crimes." The defense was once again vehemently arguing that the criminal liability of a commanding officer for the war crimes of their troops must be dependent upon personal participation of some kind in the criminal act. Nowhere in the indictment, they pointed out, was it alleged that Yamashita personally committed any of the atrocities, that he ordered their commission, or that he even had any knowledge of their commission. And, in fact, no evidence ever produced by the prosecution at the trial indicated that Yamashita had known of, or been involved in, any of the atrocities. Yamashita, his lawyers argued in the brief, could not be executed for something of which he was completely ignorant.

The defense felt that this, the second of the three areas of issue, represented Yamashita's best hopes for judicial intervention. It seemed inconceivable that a man could be hanged for what amounted, at the very most, to inefficiency.

Finally, the defense team argued that Yamashita had been denied a fair trial. First, his lawyers had been given insufficient time to prepare a defense. He had been presented with a bill of particulars listing sixty-four instances of criminal conduct a mere three weeks before trial and than a supplementary bill listing an additional fifty-nine charges at the opening of the trial. His lawyers' pleas for additional time to investigate the facts behind the allegations in order to prepare a defense had been summarily denied by the commission, and they had been forced to begin trial unprepared.

Related to this were two collateral arguments: Yamashita had been denied the right to confront witnesses and the right to have the same evidentiary rules applied to his trial as would have been applied to that of an American general. MacArthur had not only caused the indictment to be drafted against Yamashita, created the commission, appointed its members from his command, oversaw the naming of the defense and prosecution attorneys, and been the principal appeal, he had also determined what evidence would be admissible. Section 16 of MacArthur's regulations for conduct of the trial ordered that the commission should admit such evidence "as in its opinion would be of assistance in proving or disproving the charge." Thus, the commission had permitted the introduction into evidence of hearsay, opinions, conclusions, written statements, depositions—almost any conceivable thing offered—and without the usual requirements of authentication. Triple hearsay compounded by conjecture had not been uncommon. This, the defense contended, resulted in a denial of Yamashita's right to face and cross-examine the witnesses against him, a right granted to anyone accused in an American military or civil court under the due process requirements of the Fifth Amendment.

A more elaborate argument supporting this position was also set forth by Yamashita's lawyers. Both Japan and the United States were signators to the Geneva Convention of 1929. Article 63 of that Convention read: "Sentence may be pronounced against a prisoner of war only by the same courts and according to the same procedure as in the case of persons belonging to the armed forces of the detaining Power." Under the Geneva Convention, then, Yamashita was entitled to the same procedural benefits afforded American military men, and those benefits included the provisions of the Articles of War. Article 23 of those articles provided that depositions and written statements could not be introduced into evidence in a capital case. Further, Article 38 stated that military commissions must "apply the rules of evidence generally recognized in the trial of criminal cases in the district courts of the United States." Neither of these protections had been afforded Yamashita at his trial.

The defense concluded its brief by noting that the commission had violated Article 60 of the Geneva Convention as well. That section dictated that "at the opening of judicial proceeding directed against a prisoner of war, the detaining Power shall advise the representative of the protecting Power thereof as soon as possible, and always before the date set for the opening of the trial." At the time of Yamashita's trial in the Philippines, Switzerland had been designated by Japan for the protection of Japanese prisoners of war; neither country was ever notified of the trial.

The prosecution staff of eleven lawyers filed a reply brief in answer to the contentions raised by Yamashita's defense team. They opened by challenging the right of the Supreme Court to review the Yamashita case. General Yamashita was in the lawful custody of the military authorities as an enemy belligerent, they said, held under a charge of committing war crimes. His detention, therefore, involved "strictly political and military considerations" with which the Supreme Court had no right involving itself. Yamashita's trial, they argued, was a political matter, not a judicial one.

After questioning the Court's right to review the trial, the prosecution next addressed itself to the issue of the commission's jurisdiction over war crimes. This jurisdiction continues at least as long as a formal state of war exists, they argued; the critical time was not the cessation of hostilities, through armistice or surrender, but the complete peace effectuated by proclamation or treaty. And at the time Yamashita had been tried, a peace treaty had not yet been signed. Technically, a state of war still existed between Japan and the United States. Furthermore, the prosecution contended, the presidential war power from which the commission derives its existence is not limited to actual war time; the authority carries with it the inherent power to guard against the possible renewal of the conflict and to remedy the evils that war has produced.

As to the charges brought against Yamashita, the prosecution staff pointed out that the Geneva Convention imposes upon a commander a duty to take such appropriate measures as are within his power to control the troops under his command for the prevention of criminal conduct. Article 26 of the convention makes it the duty of the commanders-in-chief of the belligerent armies to "provide for the details of execution of the foregoing articles as well as see for the unforeseen cases." Unfortunately, the convention did not specify what should be done to a general who failed to perform this duty; more importantly, it failed to describe the extent of this duty. Nevertheless, the prosecution argued that Yamashita, as commanding general of the 14th Army and as governor of the Philippines, failed to take affirmative action to prevent criminal conduct by Japanese soldiers and sailors and therefore could be charged with personal responsibility.

The prosecution answered the defense contentions of an unfair trial with one simple retort: Yamashita simply had no right to a fair trial! He was not a prisoner of war, entitled to the protection of the Geneva Convention and the Articles of War, but rather a war criminal. Essentially, the government lawyers claimed that Yamashita had no procedural rights as a war criminal.

The prosecution ended its presentation by reminding the Supreme Court that any review, if permitted, was limited to jurisdictional questions. The Court could not look into the questions of whether the evidence produced at the trial was sufficient to establish guilt, whether the trial had been conducted fairly, or whether Yamashita was, in fact, even guilty!

The briefs were submitted to the nine members of the Court, and their contentions considered. January 7 and 8 were set for oral argument.

On January 7, Captain Reel, Captain Sandberg, and Colonel Clarke appeared before the nine members of the Supreme Court of the United States. The prosecution was represented by Solicitor General McGrath and Assistant Attorney General Judson. The arguments lasted for two days. Then the nine justices retired to weigh the various positions in their own minds. It was to be a month before the opinion of the Court was filed.

On February 4, 1946, the Supreme Court made public their decision: Yamashita's petition was denied. Six justices simply decided that the military had authority to conduct the trial and that the Court lacked jurisdiction to question the fairness of that trial. Justice Jackson chose to take no part in the decision, and Justices Murphy and Rutledge delivered unusually stinging dissents.

Chief Justice Stone wrote the rather brief opinion for the six-member majority. He prefaced his conclusions with a statement recognizing that "we are not concerned with the guilt or innocence of [Yamashita]. We considered here only the lawful power of the Commission to try [him] for the offense charged. . . . If the military tribunals have lawful authority to hear, decide and condemn, their action is not subject to judicial review merely because they have made a wrong decision on disputed facts. Correction of their errors of decision is not for the courts but for the military authorities which are alone authorized to review their decisions."

The chief justice then turned to each of the defense contentions, disposing of them in turn. Jurisdiction under the executive war power was clear; a state of war still technically existed between Japan and the United States at the time of trial. In any event, he reasoned, "the trial and punishment of enemy combatants who have committed violations of the law of war is. . .a part of the conduct of war." In other words, Stone was using the "bootstrap" argument: Even if hostilities had ceased, the very trial itself was a part of war—and therefore hostilities technically were continuing.

Chief Justice Stone next addressed the question of whether Yamashita could be charged in an indictment that did not allege that he either committed, directed, or knew about the criminal acts. He simply concluded, with little discussion, that there was an affirmative duty to prevent such acts and that failure of that duty would be punished.

Stone emphasized that "we do not here appraise the evidence on which [Yamashita] was convicted. We do not consider what measures, if any, [he] took to prevent the commission, by the troops under his command, of the plain violations of the law of war detailed in the bill of particulars, or whether such measures as he may have taken were appropriate and sufficient to discharge the duty imposed upon him. These are questions within the peculiar competence of the military officers composing the Commission and were for it to decide." In fact, he reminded the world for a third time in a footnote that "we do not weigh the evidence. We merely hold that the charge sufficiently states a violation against the laws of war."

Stone then turned to the government's use of normally inadmissible hearsay evidence against Yamashita and the defense position that the Articles of War prohibited it. Stone avoided this problem by simply saying that the Articles of War did not apply to enemy combatants! Furthermore, the military commission had not been convened by virtue of the Articles of War, but pursuant to the "common law of war"—a fine distinction. Therefore, the protective provisions of Articles 25 and 38 were not applicable.

But Article 63 of the Geneva Convention clearly gave Yamashita the same procedural rights as an American soldier, and an American soldier would be protected by the Articles of War: "Sentence may be pronounced against a prisoner of war only by the same courts and according to the same procedure as in the case of persons belonging to the armed forces of the detaining power." Stone disposed of this roadblock with Alice in Wonderland logic; the language, he said, referred only to offenses committed *while* a prisoner of war! With absolutely no legal or historical basis, he unilaterally bent the clear meaning of the convention's terms.

In any event, Stone once again added, "For reasons already stated we hold that the commission's rulings on evidence and on the mode of conducting these proceedings against [Yamashita] are not reviewable by the courts, but only by the reviewing military authorities."

Finally, Stone disposed of the defense contention that Switzerland, as Japan's representative, had not been advised of the trial by reasserting that the terms of the Geneva Convention applied only to persons who are subjected to judicial proceedings for offenses committed *while* prisoners of war.

In his summarizing conclusion, Stone was careful to avoid any language suggesting that the trial itself had been fairly conducted. It was lawfully convened, he wrote, and had the authority to try Yamashita for the charges enumerated. Nothing further was relevant.

But Justice Frank Murphy had distinctly different views on the trial of General Yamashita. And he wasted no time in making them very clear:

> The significance of the issue facing the Court today cannot be overemphasized. . . . The grave issue raised by this case is whether a military commission so established and so authorized may disregard the procedural rights of an accused person as guaranteed by the Constitution, especially by the due process clause of the Fifth Amendment.
>
> The answer is plain. The Fifth Amendment guarantee of due process of law applies to "any person" who is accused of a crime by the Federal Government or any of its agencies. No exception is made as to those who are accused of war crimes or as to those who possess the status of an enemy belligerent. . . . The immutable rights of the individual . . . belong not alone to the members of those nations that excel on the battlefield or that subscribe to the democratic ideology.

Murphy then angrily addressed himself to the general conduct of the trial itself:

> No military necessity or other emergency demanded the suspension of the safeguards of due process. Yet [Yamashita] was rushed to trial under an improper charge, given insufficient time to prepare an adequate defense, deprived of the benefits of some of the most elementary rules of evidence and summarily

sentenced to be hanged. In all this needless and unseemly haste there was no serious attempt to charge
or to prove that he committed a recognized violation
of the laws of war. He was not charged with personally participating in the acts of atrocity or with ordering or condoning their commission. Not even knowledge of these crimes was attributed to him. . . . The
recorded annals of warfare and the established princi-
ples of international law afford not the slightest
precedent for such a charge. This indictment in effect
permitted the military commission to make the crime
whatever it willed, dependent upon its biased view
as to [Yamashita's] duties and his disregard thereof, a
practice reminiscent of that pursued in certain less
respected nations in recent years.

Without apparent let-up Justice Murphy then analyzed
the effect of the trial with historical perspective. "The
high feelings of the moment doubtless will be satisfied.
But in the sober afterglow will come the realization of the
boundless and dangerous implications of the procedure
sanctioned today. No one in a position of command in an
army, from sergeant to general, can escape those implications. Indeed, the fate of some future President of the
United States and his chiefs of staff and military advisors
may well have been sealed by this decision."

It is interesting to note that in the tragic My Lai incident, it was Lieutenant Calley, the officer who directed
the massacre, who was tried and convicted; Generals
Westmoreland and Abrams, whose "affirmative duty" it
was to "control the operations of the members of his
command" by MacArthur's and Stone's reasoning, were
never charged with the crime.

Justice Murphy continued in his dire analyses of the
Yamashita case's place in history.

To subject an enemy belligerent to an unfair trial,
to charge him with an unrecognized crime or to vent

on him our retributive emotions only antagonizes the enemy nation and hinders the reconciliation necessary to a peaceful world.

That there were brutal atrocities inflicted upon the helpless Filipino people. . .is undeniable. . . . That just punishment should be meted out to all those responsible for criminal acts of this nature is also beyond dispute. But these factors do not answer the problem in this case. They do not justify the abandonment of our devotion to justice in dealing with a fallen enemy commander. To conclude otherwise is to admit that the enemy has lost the battle but has destroyed our ideals.

War breeds atrocities. From the earliest conflicts of recorded history to the global struggles of modern times inhumanities, lust and pillage have been the inevitable by-products of man's resort to force and arms. Unfortunately, such despicable acts have a dangerous tendency to call forth primitive impulses of vengeance and retaliation among the victimized peoples. . . .

If we are ever to develop an orderly international community based upon a recognition of human dignity it is of the utmost importance that the necessary punishment of those guilty of atrocities be as free as possible from the ugly stigma of revenge and vindictiveness.

Having given vent to his inner feelings about the case and about the context in which it occurred, Justice Murphy proceeded to analyze the contentions raised by the defense. He agreed with the chief justice that the commission had been properly constituted and had jurisdiction to try war crimes. But he then voiced his major disagreement with the majority opinion.

The charges brought against Yamashita, he said, simply did not state a recognized violation of the laws of war. Yamashita had been charged with failing to shoulder an impossible burden—controlling a broken,

confused, and dispersed army. Murphy carefully reviewed the facts leading up to the atrocities. By the end
of 1944, the island of Leyte was largely in American
hands, and in early 1945 Luzon was invaded. Yamashita
was confronted with multiple landings from MacArthur's
vastly superior forces, not to mention guerrilla activity
and General Kinney's aircraft. Yamashita's army was
forced into a piecemeal commitment; units were isolated,
morale was low, communication was broken, retreat was
everywhere, and confusion reigned. "It was at this time
and place that most of the alleged atrocities took place,"
Murphy noted. In fact, most of the atrocities were shown
at the trial to have been committed by naval personnel
assigned to Yamashita's command at the last moment,
units that Yamashita had little real control over.

Nowhere, Murphy observed, was it alleged in the
charges that Yamashita personally committed any of the
atrocities, or that he ordered their commission, or that he
had any knowledge of the commission by members of his
command. And the findings of the commission bore out
this absence of any personal involvement. Justice
Murphy continued angrily:

> In other words, read against the background of mili-
> tary events in the Philippines subsequent to October
> 9, 1944, these charges amount to this: "We, the vic-
> torious American forces, have done everything pos-
> sible to destroy and disorganize your lines of com-
> munication, your effective control of your personnel,
> your ability to wage war. In those respects we have
> succeeded. We have defeated and crushed your
> forces. And now we charge and condemn you for
> having been inefficient in maintaining control of
> your troops during the period when we were so ef-
> fectively besieging and eliminating your forces and
> blocking your ability to maintain effective control.
> Many terrible atrocities were committed by your dis-
> organized troops. Because these atrocities were so

widespread we will not bother to charge or prove
that you committed, ordered, or condoned any of
them. We will assume that they must have resulted
from your inefficiency and negligence as a commander. In short, we charge you with the crime of
inefficiency in controlling your troops. We will judge
the discharge of your duties by the disorganization
which we ourselves created in large part. Our standards of judgment are whatever we wish to make
them."

Murphy then added: "Nothing in all history or in international law, at least as far as I am aware, justifies such a
charge against a fallen commander of a defeated force. To
use the very inefficiency and disorganization created by
the victorious forces as the primary basis for condemning
officers of the defeated armies bears no resemblance to
justice or to military reality."

The elderly Supreme Court justice then pointed out
that the armed forces of the United States recognized
war-crime liability only as to those who commit the offenses or direct their commission. The War Department
publication, "Rules of Land Warfare," sets forth the principal offenses under the laws of war recognized by the
United States, and in so doing it implicitly states that
direct involvement would be necessary for punishment at
the hands of an enemy court.

Murphy then reviewed the historical precedents. He
had found numerous cases where commanding officers
were found to have violated the laws of war by specifically ordering members of their command to commit
atrocities and other war crimes. And he had discovered
others where officers had been held liable where they
knew that a crime was to be committed, had the power to
prevent it, and failed to exercise that power. But in no
recorded instance could he find a case where the mere
inability to control troops under fire or attack by superior

forces was held a basis for a charge of violation of the laws of war.

Mr. Justice Murphy closed his emotionally charged legal opinion by warning of the implications of the injustice done to Yamashita: "An uncurbed spirit of revenge and retribution, masked in formal legal procedure for purposes of dealing with a fallen enemy commander, can do more lasting harm than all of the atrocities giving rise to that spirit."

Justice Wiley Rutledge followed Murphy with an opinion no less forceful for its ponderously literate style.

> Not with ease does one find his views at odds with the Court's in a matter of this character and gravity. Only the most deeply felt convictions could force one to differ. That reason alone leads me to do so now, against strong considerations for withholding dissent.
>
> This trial is unprecedented in our history. . . . I have not been able to find precedent for the proceeding in the system of any nation founded in the basic principles of our constitutional democracy, in the laws of war or in other internationally binding authority or usage.

Rugledge then agreed with Murphy that the charges did not state a valid crime. "Mass guilt," he wrote, "we do not impute to individuals, perhaps in any case but certainly in none where the person is not charged or shown actively to have participated in or knowingly to have failed in taking action to prevent the wrongs done by others." He then noted, with some irony, that one of the charges against Yamashita had been that American soldiers had been tried and executed without notice having been given to the protecting power of the United States in accordance with the Geneva Convention; Chief

Justice Stone, of course, had ruled that the Geneva Convention did not apply, after finding the charges against Yamashita legally valid.

The dissenting justice then turned to the rules of evidence promulgated for Yamashita's trial by MacArthur. He expressed shock that a man could be convicted in a capital case on the basis of "hearsay once, twice or thrice removed, more particularly when the documentary evidence or some of it was prepared *ex parte* by the prosecuting authority and includes not only opinion but conclusions of guilty." The commission was free to consider evidence expressly excluded by the Federal Rules of Procedure, he noted.

> A more complete abrogation of customary safeguards relating to proof. . .hardly could have been made. So far as the admissibility and probative value of evidence was concerned, [MacArthur's] directive made the commission a law unto itself.
>
> It acted accordingly. As against insistent and persistent objection to the reception of all kind of "evidence," oral, documentary and photographic, for nearly every kind of defect under any of the usual prevailing standards for admissibility and probative value, the commission not only consistently ruled against the defense, but repeatedly stated it was bound by [MacArthur's] directive to receive the kinds of evidence it specified, reprimanded counsel for continuing to make objection, declined to hear further objections. . . . Every conceivable kind of statement, rumor, report, at first, second, third or further hand, written, printed or oral, and one "propaganda" film were allowed to come in.

The result of admitting all of this forbidden evidence, Rutledge said, was to effectively deny Yamashita the right to confront and cross-examine the witnesses supposedly testifying against him.

In fact, in viewing all of the procedural rights theoreti-

cally available to Yamashita, Rutledge observed that the
only right he had been granted was representation by
counsel. Rutledge praised the attorneys who had fought
so hard for their client. "Their difficult assignment has
been done with extraordinary fidelity, not only to the
accused, but to their high conception of military justice."
But he commented that even this shield had been taken
away from Yamashita by denying the lawyers any chance
to prepare an adequate defense.

Given three weeks to prepare to defend sixty-four
charges, and faced with the addition of fifty-nine more
charges at the commencement of trial, the defense had
understandably asked for continuances. Even the prosecution reluctantly admitted to the tribunal, "Frankly, sir,
it took the War Crimes Commission some three months
to investigate these matters and I cannot conceive of the
Defense undertaking a similar investigation with any less
period of time." Nevertheless, the requests for more time
were repeatedly denied.

> [This resulted in] cutting off the last vestige of ade-
> quate chance to prepare defense and imposing a
> burden the most able defense counsel could not
> bear. This sort of thing has no place in our system of
> justice, civil or military. Without more, this wide de-
> parture from the most elementary principles of fair-
> ness vitiated the proceeding. When added to the
> other denials of fundamental right, it deprived the
> proceeding of any *semblance* of trial as we know that
> institution.

Rutledge then pointed out that the language of Articles
25 and 38 of the Articles of War clearly applied to every
kind of military tribunal: "[The] language could not be
more broadly inclusive. . . . Every kind of miltary body
for performing the function of trial is covered." In any
event, he added, Article 63 of the Geneval Convention

obviously required the application of these Articles of War to General Yamashita.

Finally, Rutledge agreed with Murphy that the commission had violated the Geneva Convention by not notifying Switzerland, Japan's designated representative, of the Yamashita trial. The prosecution had countered that this did not invalidate Yamashita's conviction; it merely gave him a right to subsequent indemnity. Executed men, Rutledge dryly noted, are not much aided by postwar claims for indemnity.

Yamashita had been denied a fair trial, Rutledge said, and the due-process clause of the Fifth Amendment guaranteed him this right.

> This was not trial in the traditions of the common law and the Constitution. . . . If all these traditions can be so put away, then indeed we will have embarked upon a new but foreboding era of law. . . .
>
> It was a great patriot who said: "He that would make his own liberty secure must guard even his enemy from oppression; for if he violates this duty he establishes a precedent that will reach himself."

And so, despite the sharply worded dissenting opinions, Yamashita's appeal was denied. The majority had ruled that the army had legal authority to try the fallen general and that the Supreme Court was powerless to intervene on the question of whether the trial had been fairly conducted.

With the failure of Yamashita's appeal, of course, General Homma's hopes also disintegrated. The issues were identical; the results would be the same. Yamashita and Homma had but one path left.

MacArthur was presented the case of General Yamashita for review in February of 1946. MacArthur con-

sidered the case very briefly, then issued a terse statement for the media.

> It is not easy for me to pass penal judgment upon a
> defeated adversary in a major military campaign. I
> have reviewed the proceedings in vain search for
> some mitigating circumstances on his behalf. I can
> find none. Rarely has so cruel and wanton a record
> been spread to public gaze. Revolting as this may
> be in itself, it pales before the sinister and far reach-
> ing implication thereby attached to the profession
> of arms. The soldier, be he friend or foe, is charged
> with the protection of the weak and unarmed. It is
> the very essence and reason for his being. When he
> violates this trust, he not only profanes his entire
> cult but threatens the very fabric of international
> society. The traditions of fighting men are long and
> honorable. They are based upon the noblest of hu-
> man traits—sacrifice. This officer, of proven field
> merit, entrusted with high command involving au-
> thority adequate to responsibility, has failed this ir-
> revocable standard; has failed his duty to his
> troops, to his country, to his enemy, to mankind;
> has failed utterly his soldier faith. The transgres-
> sions resulting therefrom as revealed by the trial are
> a blot upon the military profession, a stain upon
> civilization and constitute a memory of shame and
> dishonor that can never be forgotten. Peculiarly cal-
> lous and purposeless was the sack of the ancient
> city of Manila, with its Christian population and its
> countless historic shrines and monuments of cul-
> ture and civilization. . . .
> I approve the findings and sentence of the Com-
> mission and direct the Commanding General, Army
> Forces in the Western Pacific, to execute the judg-
> ment upon the defendant, stripped of uniform,
> decorations and other appurtenances signifying mem-
> bership in the military profession.

MacArthur then added his comments on the trial—the
transcripts of which he had not bothered to read—in re-

ply to newspaper accounts which had been very critical
of the fairness of the proceedings.

> No new or retroactive principles of law, either na-
> tional or international, are involved. The case is
> founded upon basic fundamentals and practices as
> immutable and as standardized as the most natural
> and irrefragable of social codes. The proceedings
> were guided by that primary rationale of all judicial
> purposes—to ascertain the full truth unshackled by
> any artificialities of narrow method or technical arbi-
> trariness. The results are beyond challenge.

In his memoirs, MacArthur was later to comment that
the Supreme Court had approved of the conduct of the
trial by a 7-2 margin. In fact, the majority of six, not
seven, justices merely recognized the authority of the
military to conduct a trial and made a point of emphasiz-
ing that they were without jurisdiction to consider the
merits of the charges or the fairness of the proceedings.

In March of 1946, soon after Yamashita's hanging, the
case of General Homma was sent to MacArthur for a
similar review. Before he could render his decision, Captain Skeen requested permission for Homma's wife to
present personally her plea for clemency. MacArthur
consented.

Fujiko Homma appeared at MacArthur's headquarters,
unknown to her husband. A distinguished-looking older
women, Mrs. Homma spoke English fluently and exhib-
ited a grace and gentleness that reflected her aristocratic
background. At the trial she had taken the stand, and with
a quiet dignity that impressed everyone in the courtroom,
testified on behalf of her husband. One of Homma's attorneys asked her what the general's views were on the
subject of war. "He told me often that arms should be for

defense, not to attack others. His rule was never to burn people's homes, never to commit violence against civilian populations."

Seated now in the front of the man who had engineered the events leading to her husband's scheduled execution, Fujiko Homma did not plead for her husband's life. Rather, the dignified woman graciously thanked him for the consideration shown her by General Styer while she was staying in the Philippines. She expressed her deep appreciation for Styer's kindness in permitting her to visit her husband and for the sincere efforts the defense lawyers had made.

Mrs. Homma then commented that her husband was "a splendid soldier" and his death "would be a loss to the world." MacArthur curtly told her to continue, whereupon she politely requested that he read through the records of the trial. MacArthur said he would.

Fujiko Homma said, "I hear that the death sentence will be sent for your confirmation. It's a very hard job for you, I suppose." MacArthur replied in "an unpleasant and arrogant tone": "Never you mind about my job."

The elderly woman realized by his manner that this was the end of the short meeting. As she rose to leave the room, she quietly said, "Please remember me to your wife." MacArthur said nothing.

MacArthur later reflected: "She was a cultured woman of great personal charm. It was one of the most trying hours of my life. I told her that I had the greatest possible sympathy for her and understood the great sorrow of her situation. No incident, I said, could more deeply illustrate the utter evil of war and its dreaded consequences upon those like her who had little or no voice or part in it. I added that I would give the gravest consideration to what she had said."

MacArthur did consider the case. As a gesture to Mrs. Homma, he issued orders that Homma was not to be hanged, as previously ordered. Rather, he was to be shot by a firing squad.

On March 21, MacArthur again issued a statement to the American press concerning his "review" of the Homma trial.

> I am again confronted with the repugnant duty of passing final judgment on a former adversary in a major military campaign. The proceedings show that the defendant lacked the basic firmness of character and moral fortitude essential to officers charged with the high command of military forces in the field. No nation can safely trust its martial honor to leaders who do not maintain the universal code which distinguishes between those things that are right and those things that are wrong. The testimony shows a complete failure to comply with this simple but vital standard. The savageries which resulted have shocked the world. They have become synonyms of horror and mark the lowest ebb of depravity of modern times. There are few parallels in infamy and tragedy with the brutalization of troops who in good faith had laid down their arms. It is of peculiar aversion that the victims were a garrison whose heroism and valor has never been surpassed. Of all the fighting men of all time none deserved more the honors of war in their hour of final agony.

MacArthur continued his justification for the pending execution of General Homma, turning again to the critical press reporting of the trial and to the scalding opinions from Justices Murphy and Rutledge which had just reached him from the Yamashita appeal.

> In reviewing this case I have carefully considered the minority views presented by distinguished justices of the United States Supreme Court in negation not only as to the jurisdiction but as to method and spirit. . . . No trial could have been fairer than this one, no accused was ever given a more complete

opportunity of defense, no judicial process was ever freer from prejudice. . . . There were not artifices of technicality. . . . Those who would oppose such honest method can only be a minority who either advocate arbitrariness of process above factual realism, or who inherently shrink from the stern rigidity of capital punishment. . . . No sophistry can confine justice to a form. It is a quality. Its purity lies in its purpose, not in its detail.

Epilogue

THE TRIALS OF TOMOYUKI YAMASHITA AND MASAHARU Homma present a number of disturbing questions.

The validity of the establishment of trials for war crimes must be assumed. Certainly, an Eichmann, a Mengele, or a Tsuji should be held to answer for their wartime acts of inhumanity. Yet, never before—and never since—has anyone ever been convicted or executed by a victorious enemy on the grounds that they were simply negligent in commanding their military forces in the field. Never has a military leader been prosecuted for an incident when he has neither ordered, condoned, nor even been aware of the atrocity in question. It is a totally unique theory, based, in the case of Generals Yamashita and Homma, on a totally irrelevant Connecticut manslaughter prosecution.

In fact, the evidence proves conclusively that neither of the Japanese generals was even negligent, much less guilty of war crimes. These were two of the most brilliant military leaders and strategists in Japan, with long records of distinguished and honorable service. Each had

221

achieved a great victory under seemingly impossible circumstances: Homma had defeated MacArthur at Bataan
in the face of overwhelming superiority, and Yamashita
had taken Singapore after a brilliant campaign despite
Percival's three-to-one edge. Each was a military genius,
proven in the field and recognized as such by the responsibilities given them by their government. The evidence
produced at the one-sided trials indicated that neither
man was guilty of negligence. But, aside from this evidence, and accepting for the moment the dubious theory
of war crimes by negligence, is it likely that such men
would be guilty of "gross negligence" in commanding
their forces?

Certainly relevant to the case is the tragic irony that
both generals had a widely know reputation for being
opposed to the commencement of hostilities against the
United States. Both men were essentially pacifist;
Homma was even the recognized leader of the pro-
Wester faction in Japan. And these attitudes cost each
man dearly. Tojo and his staff were to recall Homma in
disgrace despite his victory because he had been "too
soft" on the Americans and Filipinos; nor was Tojo to
forget Yamashita's opposition to the war, shunting him
off to remote outposts after his stunning capture of Singapore. In addition, both were universally recognized as
men of character and honor. Is it likely that such men
would be guilty of permitting the atrocities with which
they were charged?

Perhaps more important than the issue of these men's
innocence or guilt is the question of precedent. For if
MacArthur was correct, then any military commander is
responsible for the criminal conduct in the field of his
subordinates. Neither Homma nor Yamashita were convicted of ordering the atrocities . . . or of even knowing
about them. Quite simply, they were convicted on a theory of absolute liability—as commanders, they were re-

sponsible. Yet, what are the ramifications of this new theory? Without question, General Creighton Abrams should be prosecuted under this new precedent. He was in command in Viet-Nam when Lieutenant Calley engaged in the massacre at My Lai, just as Homma had been in command when the Death March took place and as Yamashita had been technically in command when Manila was pillaged. Thomas Paine suggested that oppressing one's defeated enemy establishes a precedent that will reach oneself. Were MacArthur alive, would he suggest that General Abrams be executed for war crimes?

An even more interesting question was posed by Homma. In discussing the facts with his lawyers, the confused general asked, Who is responsible for the thousands of dead and mutilated women and children in Hiroshima and Nagasaki? Certainly, Yamashita was prosecuted for the deaths of the thousands of civilians in Manila. Should President Truman have been executed for the dropping of the atom bombs?

Another nagging question that arised from the trials of the two Japanese generals is their procedural integrity. Whether the American constitution applies or not—a debatable issue—the problem remains one of basic fairness. Certain facts are inescapable. One man caused the charges to be drafted; appointed the judges, defense attorneys and prosecutors—all of whom were subordinates and, therefore, answerable to him; created the rules of evidence and procedure; named himself the sole source of appeal; and, apparently, periodically tampered with the "judicial" process to speed up the trials. Expediency and compliance with that man's know wishes were at the heart of the trials. In fact, it is difficult to review the disgraceful proceedings without the words *railroaded* or *kangaroo court* coming to mind. Certainly, by contrast, the war crimes trials at Nuremburg and Tokyo were models of legal decorum; the judiciaries were independent, the rules of evidence and procedure were observed, and the rights of the defendants were constantly protected—to the point where the trials dragged on for years.

The formal relationship between the two Japanese generals on the one hand and MacArthur on the other has ironic aspects beyond even the obvious military ones (i.e., that Homma had been the only general to defeat MacArthur in fair combat—and with an inferior force—and that Yamashita had been technically in command of troops when MacArthur's adopted city's inhabitants were brutally savaged). For underlying the entire tragedy of these trials, the principal questions, reformulated variously into legal or military or historical language, can be put thus: "How shall a military commander act under pressure? What code shall he take to preserve his country's, his troops', and his own honor? Where, finally, does his duty lie?"

The irony is that both Homma and Yamashita could well be considered Western in their approach to this series of questions. Both were generally against war; both were soldier-citizens rather than part of a martial class; both showed personal concern for the welfare of their subordinates; and neither seemed inclined to adopt a *bushido* code that demanded unremitting aggressiveness in the face of certain disaster, fanatic obedience to unsound orders, and self-inflicted death as the prize of defeat or dishonor. Yet the implied premise of their trials was precisely their noncompliance with the *bushido* code and their unwillingness to accept responsibility for events that they had no part in and were unable to control.

This *bushido* code that hails the soldier as almost semidivine but makes of him a mere agent in the foolishness or cruelty of his superiors—and at the same time demands that he inflict the same upon his inferiors—seems much more evident in the character of MacArthur than in either Homma or Yamashita. It was MacArthur for whom inefficiency became complicity and guilt. If a soldier's right conduct was of near-infinite worth, so his wrong conduct was of near-infinite evil. Why else insist upon the death of a merely recalcitrant or inefficient enemy general? Neither in American law nor in American military tradition is such a code imposed. It was MacArthur, the *bushido* general, who imposed it, and the trial of generals recounted here involved not two but three generals—all, in one way or another, found guilty.

The trials and executions of Tomoyuki Yamashita and Masaharu Homma constituted a terrible tragedy, one that has for too long been buried in abeyance to the memory of a brilliant American military leader. Yamashita and Homma were also brilliant leaders, as well as men of character and honor. Their memories too deserve to be honored.

Just as the Nuremburg and Tokyo trials should establish the basic premise that inhumane acts during wartime will not go unpunished, so should the Manila trials now stand for the concept that war crimes trials will not be misused by conquering leaders for personal or political vendettas.

As one of Yamashita's lawyers, Captain Reel, later wrote: "No American who loves his country can read the record of the prosecution's efforts in this respect without an abiding and painful sense of shame. . . . We have been unjust, hypocritical and vindictive. We have defeated our enemies on the battlefield, but we have let their spirit triumph in our hearts."

Bibliography

Belote, James H. and William M. *Corregidor: The Saga of a Fortress*. New York: Harper & Row, 1967.

Butow, Robert J. C. *Tojo and the Coming of the War*. Princeton: Princeton University Press, 1961.

Byars, Hugh. *Government by Assassination*. New York: A. A. Knopf, 1942.

Dull, Paul S. *The Tokyo Trials*. Ann Arbor: University of Michigan Press, 1957.

Falk, Stanley L. *Bataan: The March of Death*. New York: Norton, 1962.

Fixel, Rowland. *Trial of Japan's War Lords*. n.p. 1959.

Glueck, Sheldon. *War Criminals*. New York: A. A. Knopf, 1944.

Harrison, Ernest J. *The Fighting Spirit of Japan*. New York: C. Scribners's Sons, 1913.

Hersey, J. *Men on Bataan*. New York: A. A. Knopf, 1942.

Hunt, Frazier. *The Untold Story of Douglas MacArthur*. New York: New American Library, 1964.

Ind, Allison. *Bataan the Judgment Seat.* New York: Macmillan, 1944.

James, David H. *The Rise and Fall of the Japanese Empire.* London: Allen & Unwin, 1951.

Kato, Masuo. *The Lost War.* New York: A. A. Knopf, 1946.

Keats, John. *They Fought Alone.* New York: Lippincott, 1963.

Kenworthy, A. S. *The Tiger of Malaya.* New York: Exposition Press, 1953.

Kolko, Gabriel. *The Politics of War.* New York: Random House, 1968.

MacArthur, Douglas. *Reminiscences.* New York: McGraw-Hill, 1964.

———. *Duty, Honor, Country.* New York: McGraw-Hill, 1965.

Manchester, William. *American Caesar.* Boston: Little, Brown, 1978.

Mayer, Sydney L. *MacArthur.* New York: Ballantine Books, 1971.

Morton, Louis. *U. S. Army in World War II. The War in the Pacific: The Fall of the Philippines.* Washington D.C.: Office of the Chief of Military History, Department of the Army, 1953.

Norman, Francis J. *The Fighting Man of Japan.* London: Constable & Co., 1905.

Potter, John Deane. *A Soldier Must Hang.* London: F. Muller, 1963.

Proceedings before the Military Commission Convened in the Matter of U.S. vs. Masaharu Homma.

Proceedings before the Military Commission Convened in the Matter of U.S. vs. Tomoyuki Yamashita.

Redmond, Juanita. *I Served on Bataan*. Philadelphia and New York: J. B. Lippincott, 1943.

Reel, A. Frank. *The Case of General Yamashita*. Chicago: University of Chicago Press, 1949.

Reports of General MacArthur: Japanese Operations in the Southwest Pacific Area. Volume 2, Parts I and II.

Reischauer, Edwin O. *Japan Past and Present*. New York: A. A. Knopf, 1964.

Resident Commissioner of the Philippines to the United States. *Report on the Destruction of Manila*.

Romulo, Carlos. *I Saw the Fall of the Philippines*. New York: Doubleday, Doran & Co., 1942.

Russell, Lord Edward. *The Knights of Bushido*. London: Dutton, 1958.

Sakai, Saburo. *Samurai*. New York: Ballantine Books, 1957.

Sansom, G. B. *The Western World and Japan*. New York: A. A. Knopf, 1950.

Smith, Robert Ross. *U. S. Army in World War II. The War in the Pacific: Triumph in the Philippines*. Washington: Office of the Chief of Military History, Department of the Army, U. S. Government Printing Office, 1963.

Supreme Commander for the Allied Powers. *International Military Tribunal for the Far East*. Washington: U. S. Government Printing Office, 1947.

Swinson, Arthur. *Four Samurai*. London: Hutchinson, 1968.

Toland, John. *The Rising Sun*. New York: Random House, 1970.

Wainwright, Jonathan M. *General Wainwright's Story*. Garden City, N.Y.: Doubleday & Co., 1946.

Whitney, Courtney. *MacArthur: His Rendezvous with Destiny*. New York: A. A. Knopf, 1956.

Willoughby, Amea. *I Was on Corregidor*. New York: Harper, 1943.

Yamashita v. Styer, 372 U.S. 1

Yanaga, Chitoshi. *Japanese People and Politics*. New York: Wiley, 1956.

Index